The Polish Middle Class

STUDIES IN SOCIAL SCIENCES, PHILOSOPHY AND HISTORY OF IDEAS

Edited by Andrzej Rychard

Advisory Board

Joanna Kurczewska,
Institute of Philosophy and Sociology, Polish Academy of Sciences
Henryk Domański,
Institute of Philosophy and Sociology, Polish Academy of Sciences
Szymon Wróbel,
Artes Liberales College, University of Warsaw

VOLUME 13

PETER LANG
EDITION

Henryk Domański

The Polish Middle Class

Translated by Patrycja Poniatowska

PETER LANG
EDITION

Bibliographic Information published by the Deutsche Nationalbibliothek
The Deutsche Nationalbibliothek lists this publication in the Deutsche Nationalbibliografie; detailed bibliographic data is available in the internet at http://dnb.d-nb.de.

Library of Congress Cataloging-in-Publication Data
Domański, Henryk.
  [Polska klasa srednia. English]
  The Polish middle class / Henryk Domański ; translated by Patrycja Poniatowska.
    pages cm — (Studies in Social Sciences, Philosophy and History of Ideas, ISSN 2196-0151 ; vol. 13)
  Includes bibliographical references and index.
  ISBN 978-3-631-64726-4
  1. Middle class—Poland. 2. Social classes—Poland. 3. Poland—Social conditions—1989- I. Title.
  HT690.P6D65713 2015
  305.5'509438--dc23
                         2015007524

This book was financially supported by the
Institute of Philosophy and Sociology of the Polish Academy of Sciences.

This translation has been funded by the Foundation for Polish Science.

FNP
Fundacja na rzecz
Nauki Polskiej

ISSN 2196-0151
ISBN 978-3-631-64726-4 (Print)
E-ISBN 978-3-653-04349-5 (E-Book)
DOI 10.3726/978-3-653-04349-5

© Peter Lang GmbH
Internationaler Verlag der Wissenschaften
Frankfurt am Main 2015
All rights reserved.
Peter Lang Edition is an Imprint of Peter Lang GmbH.

Peter Lang – Frankfurt am Main · Bern · Bruxelles · New York · Oxford · Warszawa · Wien

This publication has been peer reviewed.

www.peterlang.com

Table of Contents

Introduction

If you can fill the unforgiving minute
With sixty seconds' worth of distance run,
Yours is the Earth and everything that's in it.
And – which is more – you'll be a Man, my son!

Rudyard Kipling

In capitalist countries, the middle class is a basic component of the social structure. Why a component rather than a genuine "class" will soon be shown. Our main question is whether the middle class is to be found in Poland, as well. A handful of reflections to start with. It is September, 2002. Thirteen years ago, when the middle class and the appended themes of unemployment and exchange quotation were addressed in the Polish media and political debates, hardly anyone was likely to believe those notions would ever be pertinent to our realities, not to mention that few actually made any sense of them. The middle class became an issue in the early 1990s, when life in Poland gradually came to resemble that of Western societies in some respects. Survey research of the time revealed that, suddenly, 45% to 50% of all adult Poles started to regard themselves as belonging to the middle class.

Thinking about the processes of the middle class formation in Poland has developed along two distinct lines. On one hand, in the media discourse, insights are produced on the spot as politicians and opinion leaders demand instantaneous diagnoses. On the other, sociologists take their time to reflect and draw on systematic analytical findings in order to form judgments. This book was written as a contribution to the latter category. In its argument, I trace symptoms of the middle class formation, referring to findings of research based on national samples.

The middle class is linked with several social mechanisms which underpin capitalism – such as meritocracy which links the rewarding system to educational credentials, ability and talents. In Western democracies, the chief beneficiaries of these principles include highly-qualified specialists, who make up the most dynamically developing segment of the middle class. In Poland, many popular truths – such as, for example, that the standard of living is better now than under the previous regime – are hard to prove. One of the incontestable truths, in my opinion, is that the significance of meritocracy has increased considerably, as evidenced in the effect of education on income, which was steadily rising throughout the 1990s. Apart from meritocracy serving as a structural determinant of the middle class, those processes have contributed to increased inequalities in Poland and reinforced the division into the intelligentsia, entrepreneurs and "the lower classes," i.e., workers and peasants.

Consciousness is popularly said to be a "delayed outcome" of changes in the social structure. In Poland, much like in other countries, changes in attitudes materialise at a far slower pace. Comparative research in post-communist countries carried out a few years after the political and economic breakthrough (Alwin et al. 1993) reported that while the populations of Central Europe tended to blame their failures and misfortunes on politicians, the Western populations tended to be more self-reliant and ascribed their failures to their own mistakes and faults. Sociological analyses suggest that confidence in equal opportunity has pervaded American society from the very start; members of the middle class have always been level-headed and firmly believed that the essence of life lies in practical problem-solving. Faith in unrestrained possibilities bred a drive to success and individualism, which fuelled progress, but also induced attendant insecurity, risk and stress.

Productive or detrimental, the growth of individualistic orientations makes for a useful point of reference in comparing Poland and the Western countries. Reasonably speaking, individualistic attitudes should be manifest also in Poland; however, as the research I cite below indicates, self-reliance has failed to increase despite the indubitable expansion of private entrepreneurship and discernible aspirations for making a career. With this in mind, we will examine other changes in value systems. History has shown that the sober materialism of entrepreneurial individualism may go hand in hand with tolerance and liberal opinions. The middle classes were formed in struggles for democratic values against aristocracy and monarchism while their very self-interest makes them wary of equalisation programmes and campaigns, state interventionism and welfare policies. Clearly, in Poland such attitudes are mostly cherished by the intelligentsia, who share many features with "the new middle class," that is, highly-qualified specialists in what the Anglo-American parlance calls the *professions*.

In Western democracies, the second important constituent of the middle class are business people. It was in this category that "the old middle class" emerged at the verge of the market society. Let's take a glimpse into the past, at a journal kept by Nathaniel William Wraxall, an English diplomat and merchant, who travelled across Poland in 1778. Portraying the social structure of Polish society (in feudal Poland, referred to as the Commonwealth of the gentry), he wrote: "Of the intermediate rank of citizens, merchants, artisans, and mechanics, the number is so small and inconsiderable, that they may be regarded as non-existent to any beneficial purpose. In a country where commerce is in a manner extinct; manufactures, except those of the first necessity, nearly unknown; industry discouraged; arts unprotected; and only the cultivation of the ground that can be considered in any degree flourishing; the middle class of men must necessarily diminish, and be of no account" (Wraxall 1800: 32-33). Wraxall's assessment is accurate, though the critique levelled by a native of the country that was a cradle of the middle class should be put in perspective: ubiquitously, the epoch merely heralded a modernisation of the social structures with the *ancien régime* still firm across Europe. We thus have no reason for shame when comparing Poland with England of the day.

Historians are still analysing the pernicious influence of the nobility and other reasons for the weakness of the Polish bourgeoisie. Although I do not intend to probe into the past in this book, history will feature in it in so far as it helps understand why the middle class must form from the grassroots. In Poland, economic analyses of conditions for stabilising the market economy come along with reform recommendations. Such authors as Jeffrey Sachs believe that if the capitalist economy is to function, it needs "core institutions," such as private property ownership, stable and convertible currency, free international trade and foreign investments, and a solid social safety net.

The views on the feasibility of transplanting such infrastructure from the West to the East do not have to be univocal. The perspective of sociologists is specific in that when analysing social structures and people we rarely take the position of experts who formulate recommendations for reform projects. Stratification systems are so complex and contain so many unknowns that the only thing we can responsibly do is point out important processes in which people are involved, and seek to understand their causes and implications. Poland has never known an ideology such as that of the American Dream which motivates individuals to reach higher, enhances self-esteem, and makes success the main criterion of worth. An American worker always contemplates setting up his own business, which is hardly a norm in Poland. A typical Pole does not regard property as a measure of status or, at least, does not start his career path with the underlying idea of "going it alone" in business.

Briefly, the basic questions this book is driven by concern the viability of "importing" the middle class. The West is where and what we want to be. Assuming that our low GDP is a valid measure of the distance between Poland and developed capitalist societies in economic modernisation, we could view obstacles to formation of the middle class as a measure of the sociological distance, defined in terms of affluence, consumption, life style, different orientations and attitudes.

I will try to point out the indications of the middle class formation processes in Poland and identify the factors which promote or essentially impede them.

After a dozen years' worth of discussion, some issues seem trivial and simple, especially that they have already been taken on board by various authors (Wesołowski 1995; Kurczewski 1998; Słomczyński 2000; Mokrzycki 2001). Basically, I will seek to prove four theses. Firstly, I indicate specialists, higher managerial staff and business owners as the most likely candidates amongst the social categories in Poland for being major actors in the formation of a middle class in the country. Their occupational positions, university education, financial status and some other traits approximate those of the Western middle class. Secondly, I posit that the 1990s were a step forward in the process of middle class formation. The process is, of course, a gradual one, unfolding as a result of a systematic increase in consumption and affluence, with its evidence, however, barely discernible in day-to-day life. The social hierarchy witnesses an emergence of distinctive attributes of the middle class, which is reflected in a growing gap between the incomes of CEOs and specialists and the earnings of the working class. In the ideal world, the empirically recordable mechanisms would shortly be followed by a change in consciousness. But, and this is my third thesis, changes toward attitudes, life goals and value systems which are distinct for the Western middle class are ambiguous and rather slow in Poland. They ensue primarily from the changes "enforced" by the new social structures and behavioural rationality of a consumer and a recipient of market services. The word "success" does not connote the highest aspirations in life for all. Fourthly, I offer a long-term prognosis, one so evident that it can hardly be contradicted: the middle class in Poland will not emerge as an exact copy of the Western model of the middle class; rather, it will be its contextually modified species strongly affected by Polish specificities.

When I was trying to come up with a title for this book, Lena Kolarska-Bobińska told me that it must be *The Polish Middle Class*. I want to thank her wholeheartedly for that.

Chapter I: The Heartening Myth

> *Our task is to allow more people to be-*
> *come middle class. The Labour Party*
> *did not come into being to celebrate*
> *working-class people having a lack of op-*
> *portunity and poverty, but to take them*
> *out of it.*
>
> Tony Blair, *Sunday Times*, 1 September, 1996

"The middle class" is made up of such divergent categories that it cannot legitimately be called a "social class." Shopkeepers who struggle to make ends meet
have little in common with renowned surgeons and university dons, not to mention the prosperous owners of law firms and corporation managers. Telephone
operators, supermarket sales assistants, office auxiliaries, postal cashiers, waiters,
chefs and many other people in low-status jobs – they all identify with the middle
class. For Charles Wright Mills (1951), small farmers were the American middle class in the settlement epoch. What is particularly peculiar about the middle
class is the very fact of it being called a class even though it includes individuals of divergent educations, discrepant standards of living and uneven incomes,
who differ in consumer preferences and enjoy unequal esteem. The middle class
may not be a social class, but it is one of the most important elements of market
society. It mobilises for action. "The middle class" stands for effectiveness and is
a factor in social stability. If we ponder the feasibility of transplanting that notion
onto Polish soil, we must answer two questions: What is the middle class? And
what benefits and risks inhere in the role it plays in the social structure?

What Is the Middle Class?

There was a time when "the middle class" merited the name of "class" far more
than it does today. On the verge of the market society, when the feudal system was
slowly but surely fading away, it formed a small and relatively homogeneous category which became differentiated only afterwards. Chronologically speaking, the
emergence of the middle class was intertwined with the development of the capitalist labour market. The formation of the middle class was boosted by a growing
demand for new occupational roles in which recruitment was based less on social
origin than on specialist qualifications, ingenuity and ambition which demanded
courage. Those new positions and roles essentially undercut the estate structures
based on inheriting parental status: the middle class started to emerge in the milieu

of small tradesmen and crafts-workshop owners associated with the medieval guilds. Yet it received a formative thrust from the flourishing commerce, bankers, storehouse owners and all those who dealt in substantial amounts of money and never shunned the risks involved in investments in transoceanic voyages for profit and repeatedly exceeding all local confines. The rise of absolute monarchies provided another impulse as it created a demand for administration cadres, commissaries, tallymen and scribes. The new class absorbed the educated bourgeoisie – physicians, lawyers, university professors and commercial agreement signatories. From these categories, occupational groups sprouted which in the English-speaking countries were later to be referred to as *professions*, in Germany – as *Bildungsbürgertum*, and in Central and Eastern Europe – as *intelligentsia*.

The attractiveness of a notion does not necessarily overlap with its conceptual clarity, but to distinguish the middle class in its pioneering period does not pose a serious difficulty. What all its members had in common was running their own business, be it a shop, a banking house or an autonomously pursued profession. Rapid industrial development, in which novel production branches and occupational differentiation came into being, generated new property criteria and new hierarchies. Though still pyramid-shaped, the social ladder started to bulge rhomboidally to the sides in its middle regions. As the time went by, big company owners, billionaires, corporation chairmen and wealthy rentiers moved upwards from the small entrepreneur category, joining the "upper" class. Initially reserved for the aristocracy of noble birth, the upper class made room for the evolving aristocracy of capital, which grounded its claims to glory on wealth and money. In the United States, which never knew the aristocracy of blood, the new upper class was being formed by the nouveau-riche Morgans, Carnegies, Rockefellers, Fords and Fricks, all of them plebeian without exception. Simultaneously, the middle class grew diversified from within, whereby the categories of small entrepreneurs, "white collars," higher managers and "free professions" crystallised in time.

In this way, the middle class came to be a force in the historical shift which transformed the system of social relations, organisation of labour and individual customs and mentalities. As they came to take positions free from the feudal stigma of inherited status and nearly insurmountable estate barriers, people had to master behaviours expressive of the capitalist rationality and disciplined life. Given this, the middle class formation meant the emergence of new positions: as the economy was gathering momentum, it could not do without engineers, managers, specialised clerical staff and governmental administration – without competent civil servants and officers. Consequently, vacancies came to be filled by competition instead of sold to the highest bidder. Professionalism became a gauge of cultural development. And professionals who provided specialised services came to be relied on for fulfilment of everyday needs, a condition of individual wellbeing.

Positions related to the middle class could emerge only in a society of mass consumption, which invented the *mortgage* – a loan one took out to buy a house. In the wealthiest countries, such as the US and the UK, it helped people to achieve the old-fashioned ideal of "a house with a garden," redolent of the gentry's sentiments and attachment to land. As the owner-mentality spread, it proved a decisive factor in the middle class formation even though ownership against credit is specific in that it ensures a comfortable life only if the owner pays off the loan systematically. By the 1950s, a typical American middle class family possessed a freezer, a dryer, an electric stove and a car – the standard set of goods which established middle-class membership. Later, the list was extended to include air-conditioning and a lawn-mower, with motor boats, campers, European holidays and yachts taking a little more time to join them as comforts and markers of middle-class membership.

The modern occupational system is based on principles which prioritise open competition and self-reliance. Capitalism cannot exist without people instinctually driven to multiply goods. Ideally, the capitalist players abide by a set of clear rules. Firstly, everybody has equal opportunities for achievement, irrespective of their social background, race or sex. The equal-opportunities postulate fares better in some countries and rather worse in other ones, yet that it diverges from reality does not disqualify it as an apt account. Secondly, success should result from individual capabilities and efforts. With the *fair play* principle in place, cheating, scheming, favouritism, nepotism, violence and coercion are forbidden. Thirdly, positions and posts of unequal importance should be accordingly rewarded. By definition, rewards are conferred proportionately to occupational qualifications and skills, that is, to individual investments and dedication. And, fourthly, while success is a fair reward, failure should be viewed as a deserved punishment dealt out by the system, which castigates a lack of courage, incompetence, sloth and deficient aspirations. Popularly phrased, it boils down to stating that our failures and successes are entirely up to us. It is everybody's duty to give it their all, self-pity is a disgrace, and to moan or blame bad fortune defies decency – this message, which profoundly affects individual thinking, is by no means stress-relieving.

Whether these rules are actually observed is quite another matter. Americans learn them in infancy, when – as Margaret Mead (1942) claims – they hear their mothers' tender "I will love you," followed by a far less tender "only if you achieve as much as other people's babies." Their growing up is suffused with a disturbing awareness of being assessed in terms of success, where love and acceptance, never guaranteed, cannot be taken for granted. "The spirit of capitalism" identified by Max Weber in the enterprising members of the emergent middle class is currently being replaced by the notion of self-acquisitiveness, a distinctive feature of particularly resourceful individuals. As the individual was granted primacy over the group, the evaluation criteria applied in the occupational domain were transposed onto other spheres of life. People grew accountable for themselves – they started to choose spouses, acquaintances, religion and opinions all by themselves. Upon graduation, they leave their parental homes in the belief that everybody must determine their future on their own. The democratic system particularly emphasises the freedom of political opinion and gatherings unfettered by censorship.

As an inevitable offshoot of rivalry, the society of equal opportunities has developed a reluctance to helping. In a system which promotes self-reliance, one who keeps investing energy and time to become a man of success will think twice before deciding to deplete his resources. And financial support to parents or children is no exception to that rule. The advantages of neighbourly help are appreciated, but within certain boundaries; a transgression beyond these limits is construed as an intrusion upon one's privacy. Asking for a loan may be deemed an inadmissible indiscretion, because such a request proves beyond reasonable doubt that one is unable to solve one's problems. In some regions of the United States (certainly including some cities on the North-Eastern coast), people greet strangers with a pleasant "good morning," a practice upheld in Poland only by hikers in the mountains. Yet this is just a ritualistic gesture, their smiling faces notwithstanding. The middle classes in their efforts to control multiple pressures, combine displays of kindness and respect with obsessive discipline and the observance of entrenched norms.

In the traditionally structured systems, obligations toward families or clans, bound by kinship, age and/or sex, were by nature diffuse because formalized, law-codified give-and-take transactions did not apply to them. Obtaining a favour entailed a requital, but when reciprocating one was not expected to say "enough, I've done my due, we're even now" upon the pain of custom violation. In contrast, the market-based systems precisely define the scope of rights and duties attributed to social roles. Rationality makes new societies precisely assign certain tasks to certain roles (if a machine tool operator is amiss in his standard tasks, substantial losses may be incurred), and obligations of the parties involved are formally regulated by contractual provisions. Recruitment to most occupational positions is based on formal requirements related to mandatory qualifications, while the employer remunerates the services rendered by the employee within clearly circumscribed limits.

The society of equal opportunities and open competition is a site of inevitable failures since the promotion of some entails setbacks for others. Failure to secure an attractive job at the onset of one's occupational career is likely to reduce future prospects for a good job as every consecutive employer will take it that the candidate previously turned down is inadequate, while the candidate will be put off from making further efforts because the first failed attempt heralds subsequent failures and increases the risk of elimination, so it seems a better solution to give up at once. The system purposefully produces a sense of insecurity since it sustains its effectiveness. An account of a typical drama of degradation could start like this: he was director at a big company, everybody bowed to him, he looked out on the world through the windows of an air-conditioned office, he had money, power and connections. All of a sudden all of it vanished, and with it friends and his exclusive club membership. He was downgraded or perhaps made redundant, and his present life suffocates and enrages him.

The capitalist market mechanisms seem like "the law of the jungle" only to those uninitiated into the Western value system. Many of those who lose cling to the belief that they are not the only victims of cruel fate, and that their failure is not an outcome of systemic ruthlessness, but rather a fair verdict. Even failures can make you stronger, people think – there is always another chance: "I was a director, I lost my job, I'm a salesman for now, but one day I may find a way to bounce back." In Poland, downfalls of this kind seem more cushioned; as lucrative jobs are scarcer, the sidetracked losers are less conspicuous. The career curve climbs less steeply perhaps, but certainly involves fewer dips.

The Middle Class and Its Psychological Role

Middle-class membership endows a sense of superiority, demanding at the same time that tokens of success be constantly displayed. It symbolises life achievement translated into a banking account, a house and relatively high income – the booty available to the perseverant ones. Simultaneously, however, it means a constant pressure to keep proving one's success to oneself and others. Belonging to the successful produces an obligation to act, an obligation which is addictive. The mechanism promotes effectiveness because it compels individuals to improve professional qualifications, accumulate wealth and seek continual development. The prosperous middle class is one of the economic driving forces of

Western societies, which is enjoyed, albeit unevenly, by all their citizens. That is why it is still a goal and an object of aspirations for Poland.

The middle class also produces a few other benefits. Besides satisfying the need for superiority, it is a factor in dispelling doubts and relieving tensions. When the pressure to succeed is considerable, ambitions are likely to exceed the actually available advancement opportunities. Yet for the majority of the US citizens, it is evident that democracy is the most rational system; the noble postulate of *let the best men win* mobilises energy, invigorates, stimulates activity and enhances productivity, which President Thomas Woodrow Wilson aptly captured in his pompous declaration that "democracy releases energies of every human being." Abraham Lincoln was born in a one-room log cabin, and Andrew Carnegie, the founder of steel industry, was a son of a poor Scottish handloom weaver – these are the favourite vignettes from the American national gallery, snapshots that fuel the imagination.

When inscribed in the ideology of equal opportunities, everybody can legitimately believe that, if not born a millionaire, they will certainly become millionaires in the future. Everybody searches, more than that, feels obliged to search for the signs of hidden natural endowments. A child raised in New York's slums can afford to entertain the idea of becoming an Eddie Murphy or a Michael Jordan. An average citizen is fed with edifying examples of mind-boggling careers and incredible strokes of luck: "I'd never have thought that it might happen to me, too, one day" is a customary line an overjoyed American spurts out on winning a lottery and turning millionaire overnight.

Such pressures affect all ambitious people, particularly those who have already registered some achievement. The other, admittedly far more numerous, category comprises those punished by the market system – those who have failed to show talent and substantiate their claims to success. The ideology generates contempt for losers and sanctions exploitation of those considered inferior. Such sentiments would be disastrous but for the middle class. The middle class, namely, relieves the tension to a degree since it offers positions attainable by all. Middle-class membership allows celebrating moderate success in tune with expectations of the majority. Not everybody must be a Bill Gates – rivalry is curtailed at a safe level and doubts alleviated.

Negative Aspects

Marx's pessimistic prediction that capitalism would bring about proletarisation and, ultimately, a demise of the middle class has not come true. The middle class makes up the most populous segment, comprising at least two thirds of Western societies. We could say that it holds up a mirror for all of their citizens. Current pronouncements about affluence, materialism, modernity, decadence or the dearth of morals of Western societies pertain largely to their middle class. Its members embody the most widespread attitudes, behaviours, consumption patterns, culinary preferences and tastes. And locating the middle class does not require the ethnological expertise of an anthropologist exploring the traces of primordial Amazonian cultures.

Attending to the attractions of the middle class, we should not lose track of its less propitious aspects. Ever since it was born, the middle class has invited criticism from the aristocracy and nobility – its rivals for prestige, economic influence and power. As they saw it, a throng of boorish, garlic-reeking parvenus heralded the downfall of culture and elites. Current criticism involved in reflection on the crisis plaguing developed market societies highlights the downsides of the individualism and materialistic orientations intrinsic to the middle classes and, at the same time, bewails the dilution of these very properties. This incompatibility of notions diminishes the merit of the argument.

Joseph Schumpeter (1995) was one of the first analysts to observe that the middle classes' interest in work, capital accumulation and investments for profit was dwindling. In his famous essay "Capitalism, Socialism and Democracy" written in the 1930, Schumpeter registered disturbing symptoms of a decrease in motivation for hard work, a slackening of self-discipline and a decline of rigorousness, all of which he attributed to an unproductive consumption drive. Later critics pointed to other implications suggested in his observations. In the second half of the 20th century, the world's wealthiest countries witnessed an unprecedented growth which made dreams of abundance attainable. A steady rise in the standard of living was accompanied by a growing desire to reap the fruit of prosperity, which though not condemnable in itself, was censured for diverting people from their proper tasks. Such anxiety found its most thorough expression in the work of Daniel Bell (1976), the proponent of the thesis of cultural contradictions inherent in capitalist society. He posited that the traditional system of values intertwined with the Protestant ethics, which underpinned the market economy, had found itself challenged by the drive for pleasure, which abrogated long-term thinking, undermined focus on occupational success and loosened morals. Capitalism had arrived at a critical point beyond which the mechanisms which induced consumption needs, i.e. the original driving force of market society, were inevitably to lead to its erosion.

Let us focus on the pitfalls of individualism. The middle class was envisaged as a spontaneous movement of small farmers, artisans and citizens united by a sense of community – that was the vision President Lincoln cherished when he called the Ohio volunteers about to depart for the battlegrounds of the Civil War the very epitomes of the American middle class (Quirk i Bridwell 1992:3). An inclination toward self-reliance, by the way, does not preclude a sense of community – the Protestant religion is informed by the idea that success testifies to moral superiority, in the sense that it proves that individual talents have been fully employed in furthering the common good. It is only inordinate individualism that has come under sharp critique as a negative manifestation. The authors of books which feature "unity of hearts" in the titles and explore threats that beset the world – such as Lasch (1982), Harrington (1983), Bellah (1986), Etzioni (1994) or Derber (1996) – argue that individualism destroys family life, kills the spirit of neighbourliness and imperils fundamental values. For them, 19th-centrury capitalism was more mindful of these values in promoting social harmony, solidarity and virtues superior to effectiveness and profit. When tackling such fundamental problems, it is impossible to assess the diagnostic merit of such opinions univocally, especially since catastrophic judgments are difficult to distinguish from hard facts. *Habits of the Heart*, a book by Bellah et al., underscores that the ethics in which "the spirit of capitalism" was steeped tends to be replaced in individualism by narrow-minded pragmatism and economic utility. Simultaneously, the authors point out that self-discipline, a sense of duty and respect for authority are vanishing while "unbridled" self-promotion is rampant. Bellah (1986) explains that "in the middle-class societies individual freedom became religion; however, abuse of this value undermines sense of democracy; in effect the bough we are sitting on became shaky, if it was not cut."

It is not my task here to present a complete list of the psychoneurotic complaints of the middle class; nor is it to discuss in-depth the cultural contradictions analysed by Bell. Mental tensions are a distinctive characteristic of the social categories which have got rid of material exigencies, but stumbled upon spiritual ones attributable, in all probability, to prioritisation of self-realisation and a chase after positive feedback. Undeniably, members of developed capitalist societies have shown the world what price individuals pay for the successes of the market economy. Today, more and more voices are heard appealing to restore to the middle classes their faith in success, equal opportunity and healthy rivalry – the groundwork of the republican system with its democratic elections and appointment of talented individuals to key offices. The authors proclaiming the crisis of capitalism advocate action for alleviating the middle classes' vulnerability and restoring their sense of self-efficacy.

In Poland, however, the point lies in creating the middle class, rather than in "restoring" it. Intense propagandist work has been engaged in for this purpose by politicians and the media, reminiscent somewhat of the attempts to create a heroic image of the working class under the previous regime. In the early 1990s, such action was organised and headed mainly by the government and President Wałęsa, who repeatedly called upon business circles; journalists, in their turn, accused society of immaturity and passivity vis-à-vis change. Interestingly, none of the successive cabinets, parties, trade unions and other agencies questioned the necessity to support the middle classes, which was quite a feat, considering how conflicted the political and social environment was at that stage. Championing the middle class became an element of political correctness among the elites. The seeds of good will, however, fell on inhospitable ground because in a country of such low living standards as Poland one could hardly find an equivalent of the British or American "middle class."

As history has shown, the development of the middle class follows a certain pattern. First of all, certain occupational positions must emerge alongside specific recruitment, promotion and payment mechanisms typical of the capitalist labour market. In the second stage, a new mentality must evolve with its concomitant life style and attitudes. And as it is easier to found institutions than to foster consciousness, the process is a long one and abounds in quirky shifts and turns. The dynamics of the changes initiated by the fall of communism give us a chance to observe the unique phenomenon of new social categories being formed over but a dozen years, a pace nothing short of incredible by sociological standards.

The analyses I include in this book sum up the first of these stages. They concentrate on "the middle class" as an indicator of transformations which involve the formation of new social hierarchies and a reshaping of the existing categories, such as upper managers, the intelligentsia, owners, workers and peasants. They are supposed to substantiate the claim that over the less than twenty years since the Round Table negotiations the social hierarchy has undergone essential changes in its basic dimensions, that is, in occupational structure and income distribution. Specifically, many new occupational roles have emerged and incomes have come to depend strongly on the level of education and actual performance. The rewarding system was first to respond to the newly introduced market mechanisms, which put a premium on high qualifications, capacities and talents. This is an optimistic observation which bodes well for the future. In Polish society, phenomena related to the "middle class" may, though need not, foster a modernisation of social relationships. That the new generation of the Polish intelligentsia buy a house to mark their transition into adulthood does not suffice to justify the thesis of a rise of the middle class in Poland.

Chapter II: Consumption, Affluence, New Style and New Structures

It matters not how straight the gate,
How charged with punishments the
scroll, I am the master of my fate:
I am the captain of my soul.

William Ernest Henley, "Invictus"

The main indicators of middle class status are: ownership, a good job, affluence and life style.

Ownership is the foundation of middle-class society. Having a business, capital or rare expert qualifications demanded by the labour market makes a difference – owners are inclined to regard their efforts and look to the future with greater confidence and self-reliance. In big cities, traffic jams have become an unanticipated offshoot of the development of the market society: driving downtown along Wybrzeże Gdańskie (a street in Warsaw), one can experience a sense of community with other car owners. Endorsement of the same rules and affinity of beliefs are distinctive traits of the specific category assembling owners of vehicles, houses and apartments, means of production, commodities and other forms of property – ownership as such does not make them a separate "class," but it definitely singles them out from other social categories. Nothing comes anywhere near ownership in terms of motivating effort, hard work and investments in self-development. And few things offer gratification matching that of a growing banking account and occupational advancement. So far, no better way has been invented to instil self-discipline, belief in stability, regard for the social order, support for democracy and commitment to orderliness. People who own something feel free and start to act differently.

Closely related to, though not synonymous with, ownership is another characteristic of the middle class – affluence and a high standard of living. In England, few factors have enhanced the middle class's sense of superiority to the masses more emphatically than the high income tax levied by William Pitt in 1792 to raise funds for the war against France. Interpreted as an authentication of the capacity to bear burdens for the country, the tax substantiated claims to prestige and sanctioned the citizenship of the middle class. Property, income and other benchmarks of material status attest to membership in the middle class if they exceed a certain decent level, which is, of course, relative and depends on a particular context. In 1990, 59% of American families owned a house, and in 1998, 54% had two cars (Hacker 1998: 61).

As for Poland, the affluence of the intelligentsia in the gray realities of communism never matched that enjoyed by the American professionals. And we are not talking of a mere difference but rather of a gaping divide, which precluded the Polish intelligentsia ever attaining middle-class status despite their comparable position in the social structure. Admittedly, over the past few decades the intelligentsia's incomes have clearly surpassed those of the lower classes (workers and peasants), not to mention its higher social prestige and cultural capital.

The third attribute of the middle class is its location in the occupational system. Because social classes are ensembles of positions, and positions are entities arm more readily available for study than banking accounts, the constitutive attributes of the middle class are occupational positions and roles. In Western societies, the demographically vast and socially diversified middle class includes white collars on the one hand and middle and small business people on the other. Long-term tendencies in the development of the occupational structure lead to the growing proportion of these categories relative to the "lower classes."

Finally, middle-class members are recognised in daily life by their appearance, life styles, values and attitudes. Admittedly, the middle class has many shortcomings and vices ascribed to it, but there is no denying that in contemporary Western democracies, it embodies the dominant, modern and appreciated patterns. For the lower classes, it is "a goal worth pursuing," while for all strata it stands for moderation, desirable wellbeing and equal opportunities, features which shield it against allegations of both destructive leftist radicalism and detached aloofness towards the masses. Even if the middle classes remain a symbol of superiority, often associated with selfishness and the relentless pursuit of success, they are on the whole considered incomparably more amiable than the elites. Middle-classness connotes the familiar local colour, inducing positive feelings.

The attributes of the middle class are a unique combination of factors produced over several centuries of the history of market societies. As citizens of a country which is trying to make up for many neglects, some of them dating back to the remote past, we are confronting the imperative to develop the middle class, without which capitalism cannot advance. Let us see which of its elements we have succeeded in acquiring over the several years of transition to a market society and which of them are still missing and why.

Directions of Changes

In February 1975, Edward Heath lost leadership of the Conservative Party, his position seized by Margaret Thatcher, probably the most ardent advocate of middle-class interests in 20th-century British politics. Four years later, Thatcher became Prime Minister and immediately went on to enact a program patently informed by and promoting the traditional bourgeois values of individualism, pursuit of success and self-reliance.

At that time, Polish promoters of liberalism – such as Mirosław Dzielski, Lech Mażewski, and Janusz Korwin-Mikke – who shared similar beliefs were few and far between. The ideology of the middle class became something more than just a vision contemplated by an isolated handful of dissidents only after the collapse of the communist system. The so-called Gdańsk liberals, represented by Jan K. Bielecki (Prime Minister in 1990-1991) and Janusz Lewandowski (later a minister), had an important say in the first non-communist government headed by Tadeusz Mazowiecki. The state and its political elites keenly engaged in constructing capitalism from scratch. This was a peculiar feature of the post-communist transformations which set them apart from all the previous ones, especially from the Western transition to the capitalist system. The Central-European variety was a commissioned, customised capitalism – "capitalism by design" as labelled by the theoreticians of the formation of the market system in Central Europe (Stark 1992; Offe 1996).

Let us take a look at the facts. The available data on transformations in the occupational structure, the standard of living and the structure of ownership provide preliminary information on how Poland fared in adjusting to the models of middle-class society.

The changes in the proportion of private entrepreneurs cast some light on how private property developed. If owning a business is an indicator of the middle class, the 1990s witnessed steps being made in the right direction. According to national surveys carried out in 1989-1999, the category of owners (outside agriculture) increased from 3.5% to 6.6% of the entire population. The rapid pace of the changes is as notable here as the absolute values of growth in this category. Arguably, 6.6% does not equal the figures for leading capitalist societies, but it does not trail very far behind, either. In the most advanced market societies, the relative proportion of business people among all the actively employed has stabilised at 10%-15% over the last fifty years. In the UK, for example, the proportion of owners amounted to 8%, in the USA – to 9%, and in Italy – to as much as 22.2% (Wright 1997: 124–127). In this respect, we have been steadily closing the gap *en route* to the middle-class society over the last ten years.

Poland was the only communist country in Central and Eastern Europe where agriculture had avoided collectivisation. This explains a less dynamic expansion of the private sector relative to the overall economy, though even here a considerable growth cannot be denied. According to the Central Statistical Office (GUS), the percentage of employment in the private sector – wage labourers and business owners considered jointly with farm-owning peasants – grew from 45.1% in 1990 to 70.2% in 1998. The public sector systematically shrank: it employed but 29.8% of the total population in 1998 ("Rocznik Statystyczny" [Statistical Yearbook] 1999: 100). By 1998, state-owned companies undergoing privatisation accounted for 70% of the total number of state-owned companies registered as of 30 July, 1990. Also the investments of the private sector exceeded those of the state-owned companies. In 1997, their shares in the investments stood at 53.4% and 46.6%, respectively, while in 1995 – only two years earlier – the public sector still dominated with 55.8% of the total investments. Apparently, private ownership developments offered solid grounds for the rise of the middle class.

Marx, "a genuine child of his century" according to Ralph Dahrendorf (1959: 48), seems to have overlooked the role of intellectual capital, professional expertise and managerial skills as a form of property. The direction of changes in these "capitals" can be most credibly established by checking whether after the debacle of the communist system higher education and managerial skills exerted a stronger impact on financial rewards. If the association between those variables increased, it would mean that the distribution of income "properly" responded to the systemic changes. In order to find that out, I compared these associations for consecutive years between 1982 and 1998, after controlling for the impact of other variables (such as social origin, sex, age or place of residence), to establish the net effects of higher education and managerial positions. The detailed findings of these comparisons are to be found in my book *Hierarchie i bariery społeczne w latach 90-tych* (*Social hierarchies and barriers in the 1990s*) (Domański 2000a).

The findings led to three conclusions which may be recapitulated under three headings. Firstly, over all those years, a university degree always guaranteed better financial advantages than primary or secondary education. This was true even in 1982. 1982 stands as a meaningful point here because in that year the principle of rewarding people for educational credentials was harshly tested in the so-called small economic reform which covered the payment system. As a by-product of the reform – implemented by the communist government just one month after martial law was imposed in Poland – the relationship between education and income was entirely unsettled. For the first time in Poland's post-war history, the Central Statistical Office reported that, on the average, white-collar salaries were lower than blue-collar wages. Financial increments to university education recorded an all-time low; nevertheless, the logic of social stratification mechanisms withstood the severity of the test in the following years.

Secondly, the overall direction of changes is clear. Ever since 1982, higher education has entailed increasingly higher incomes. In the noteworthy year of 1982, the net premium for higher education amounted to 16% as compared with the incomes of post-secondary school graduates and higher education drop-outs (i.e., after controlling for the impact of other variables affecting income). In 1987, it grew to 18%, reaching 28% in 1995 and 27% in 1998. Throughout, the difference between the categories was a conspicuous one.

The income differential between the outermost categories implies that the educational hierarchies produce growing inequalities. In 1982, net incomes of university graduates were 14% higher, while those of people with primary school education 10% lower than the average income. This renders a difference of no less than 24 percentage points. In 1987, the gap increased to 41% and continued to rise progressively throughout the early 1990s to reach 65% in 1998. The growth of the income differential was steady and, we could stay, linear.

Thirdly, the rewards offered by managerial positions grew as well. This was a relevant tendency as a managerial/supervisory job is one of the essential attributes of middle class membership. Holding any position of this kind, be it a foreman, a director or a minister, entailed increasingly improved earnings. Whereas in 1982 managers' pay exceeded the average income only by 17% and in 1987 by 14%, in 1998 the difference reached the substantial 37%. Clearly, as the economic and political transformations progressed, the financial situation of managers radically improved. The managerial attributes which deserve considerable "rewards" include organisation skills, a decision-making aptitude and the burdens involved in the function, such as accountability for subordinates and constant monitoring of performance. The growing value of managerial positions in Poland seems to reflect the actual dynamics of the market forces. It proves apparently that misguided investments in managers are a lesser evil than an altogether lack of material incentives for talented and entrepreneurial individuals to seek supervisory positions.

Looking at the occupational structure, one can most clearly pinpoint changes in the social structure and, particularly ascertain whether the middle class is growing and the lower class is shrinking. Following the distinction proposed by Gustaw Schmoller (1897), one should differentiate between the "old" and the "new" middle classes. The old middle class was comprised of tradesmen, craftsmen and business people who had clustered into a distinct segment of the social structure as early as in the Middle Ages. "The new middle class," in turn, included a broad category of rank-and-file sales and services, clerks, highly-qualified specialists and the managerial staff of companies and state institutions. At the *fin de siècle*, when Schmoller formulated his long-term predictions, few expected that new middle class to become the most populous category in the occupational structure. But with the onset of the 20th century, its development gathered momentum. Having outdistanced workers and agricultural categories in an unprecedented progress, white-collars made up more than 50% of the population of capitalist countries in the 1970s. Within that internally diversified "class," the most expansive groups are, characteristically, lawyers, doctors, engineers, university professors and executives. They occupy the highest positions which involve complex occupational tasks and responsibilities, and deserve a corresponding remuneration.

Let us take a look at Poland. The increasing number of owners hardly comes as a surprise as capitalism relies on private property for its operations. Given certain optimistic, though not unfounded, assumptions, it could be expected that the modernisation of the occupational structure would not slow down and other categories would also increase numerically. The formation of the "new middle class" would be heralded by a growth in the ranks of managerial staff and professionals, called the intelligentsia, assuming that, like in Western societies, these positions, which require the "capitals" of expertise and managerial skills, would sooner or later breed the desired orientations, attitudes and life styles.

Only modest predictions are legitimate at this point. There are no signs of a growth in the higher occupational positions that are associated with the new middle class in Western societies. The data from research carried out between 1982 and 1999 on national samples showed only an increase in the relative proportion of the non-technical intelligentsia – lawyers, doctors, university professors, secondary school teachers, economists, authors and artists (Table 1). In 1982-1995, the category accounted for 3.2–3.3% of the population, reaching 4.5% in 1999. The percentage of managerial staff in companies was actually higher in the years before the collapse of the previous regime: in 1987 it stood at 1.8%, while in 1994–1995 it dropped to 1.6%, and continued to decrease, reaching an all-time low of 1% in 1998–1999. As for the technical intelligentsia (primarily engineers), their proportion decreased systematically between 1982 and 1999, dropping from 3.1% to 2.4%.

Table 1: Changes in the distribution of socio-occupational categories

Occupational and social categories	1982	1987	1994–1995	1998–1999
Higher managerial staff and administrative officials	0.9	1.8	1.6	1.0
Non-technical intelligentsia	3.2	3.3	3.2	4.5
Technical intelligentsia	3.1	2.6	2.7	2.4
Technicians	7.0	6.2	4.6	6.0
Mid-ranked administrative staff	9.6	10.7	9.5	11.2
Clerical workers	5.0	4.6	3.9	3.5
Owners of businesses	1.6	3.6	6.2	6.6
Sales and services	6.4	7.7	10.6	10.3
Foremen	2.1	2.3	1.8	1.9
Skilled workers	25.7	26.3	27.4	24.8
Unskilled workers in production	5.8	5.7	7.0	7.2
Unskilled workers in services	4.3	3.9	6.0	6.4
Agricultural workers	1.8	1.5	2.0	2.1
Farm owners	23.5	19.8	13.4	12.2
Total	100.0	100.0	100.0	100.0

Clearly, managers and the technical intelligentsia failed to qualify as a dynamic driving force of development, with a slow-down in the expansion of these categories proving a serious problem not only in Poland. International comparative research carried out in Central and Eastern Europe in 1993 and 1994 shows that the proportions of the "new middle class" steadily declined in the Czech Republic, Slovakia, Hungary and Russia over the first half of the 1990s. (Domański 2000: 17–19). One can hardly determine whether this implies a temporary standstill or a long-term regression. Still, there is no denying that it represents a rather unexpected departure both from the predictions of modernisation theories and from the processes long observed in Western societies. One explanation is that a transition from the centrally commanded economy to the market system drastically reduced the demand for managers and engineers in the industrial sector and eliminated some traditional branches. The capitalist labour market may not have incorporated the surplus produced by socialism's grand construction projects.

Somewhat contradicting the logic behind the modernisation of the occupational structure, the strongest impulses for generating middle-class positions came from the business. These changes notwithstanding, the core of the formation of middle-class society in Poland resides in the overall transformations of the occupational structure, which have brought it closer to the structure typical of modern market societies. Apart from the phenomena noted above, the following were integral to Western societies: a decrease in the percentage of manual workers, an increase in the proportion of white collar workers and a decline in the share of farmers, making up 2%–4% of the total population.

In Poland, the equivalent processes gathered some speed at the onset of the transformation to a market society. Following owners, sales and services workers were the second most expansive segment in the occupational structure. The relative share of the group, comprised mostly of sales assistants, and also telephone operators, postal clerks and catering staff, grew from 6.4% to 10.3%. The countervailing tendency was a relatively high percentage of skilled manual workers – the evidently prevalent category, which in 1998-1999 accounted for 24.8% of the total labour force. For the advocates of modernisation, skilled workers are merely relics of the old system – an overblown and redundant vestige of the centrally planned economy, which in promoting industrial development kept boosting up vocational schooling, feeding the ranks of the working class.

Farm owners, despite a marked decrease, made up the next largest category, second only to skilled workers and resistant to decline. The proportion of the peasant class dropped from 23.5 do 12.2% of the total workforce, with the most considerable reduction recorded in the early years of the market economy development. Peasants still remain a bulwark of tradition, but such a pronounced drop in their relative proportion in the occupational structure is a good predictor for the formation of middle-class society. The third largest segment consists of mid-ranked administrative workers. In the period under analysis, the category, including among others accountants, nurses, junior managers and primary school teachers, made up 9%–11% of the population, revealing thereby a minor, but steady development. As for the lowest clerical workers (file clerks, suppliers, bank cashiers and secretaries), their proportion decreased from 5% to 3.5%. The Polish equivalents of the lowest-ranked white-collar category in developed Western societies remain the least populous group of the "new middle class" in the broad sense of the term. The only thing of notice concerning technicians is that the group registered alternating boosts and falls, which, however, were not substantial enough to trigger significant flows in the occupational hierarchy. Unskilled workers in production and services are an interesting case. Doomed to extinction by modernisation theorists, this category, including janitors, cleaners, storehouse workers, road workers and auxiliary workers in factories and construction sites, grew from 6% to 7% in the 1990s, instead of receding to make room for new occupational roles. Summing up, there were some pivotal points in the socio-occupational structure where stagnation seemed to be not only anchored, but also alarmingly entrenched. At the same time, modernisation took place as well, particularly in the growing proportions of business owners, the non-technical intelligentsia and services workers, with a concomitant decrease in the percentage of farmers.

It was only in the 1940s that American society succeeded in overcoming the Great Depression. Western Europe started enjoying similar prosperity in the 1950s, and ever since then the development of middle-class societies has been identified with a commonly felt improvement of living standards. Harold Macmillan's famous *You have never had it so good*, a dictum which encapsulated the Conservative Party's third consecutive electoral victory, is one of the maxims history is not likely to forget. In his 1957 Bedford speech, Macmillan could legitimately reason that the British should be fully confident in their government, as it was the only representative of bourgeois values and middle-class interests since liberal authority had suffered a demise.

In 1950, Poland and Spain had approximately the same income per capita in US dollars. Between 1955 and 1988, it grew from $755 to $1,860 in Poland, while in Spain it increased a dozen times more than in Poland, from $561 to $7,740 in the corresponding period. For Poland, the 1990s started with a crisis, which was followed by stabilisation and an improvement of financial indicators expressing the dynamics of the population's real incomes. The Central Statistical Office data show that by 1993 real incomes had been dropping steadily and in 1993 saw a further decrease by 2.9 per cent as compared with 1992, which, by the way, was not paralleled by a concurrent decrease in the standard of living since under the communist system most goods could hardly be purchased anyway.

In 1994, a reverse tendency took off, with the real income index rising by 0.5% – a long awaited breakthrough was in the making. 1996 was a peak year, with the average income rising by 8.9%. The second half of the 1990s witnessed a continued growth, though its rate slowed: in 1997, the average monthly income increased by 6.9% and in 1998, by 4.9%. The estimates for 2000 predicted an increase of less than 3%, but it must be remembered that the official statistics do not include the black economy, whose figures cannot be found in tax declarations – who, we could ask, keeps buying those luxury cars and villas? Evidently, the group whose incomes fall into the highest tax bracket is far more numerous than the PIT [Personal Income Tax] return forms indicate. Only this can explain the paradox of why a remarkable demand for expensive apartments and building land persists, despite the statistically documented poverty of the Polish taxpayers.

In 1999, a record number of 638,000 new cars were bought in Poland, even though, according to tax return forms, only 270,000 people had gross annual incomes over $20,000, the lower limit of the highest tax bracket. In 1999, the total tax credit for construction or purchase of a new home granted to taxpayers in the lowest income bracket amounted to nearly PLN 2 billion, nearly twice the sum granted to taxpayers in the highest income bracket (1.1 billion). The data of the Ministry of Finance imply that in 1999 only slightly more than 1% of taxpayers paid the 40% tax rate (the highest tax bracket: 270,000 taxpayers). As many as 95% of taxpayers were in the lowest tax bracket, a proportion which might confirm capitalism's wolfish nature, with an abyss between the destitute millions at the bottom and a narrow, opulent elite at the top. However, there are indications that the income pyramid in Poland has a far narrower base and a wider middle than officially reported incomes would suggest, while quite a number of middle-class wannabes are hiding below the inflated poverty limit.

Unsurprisingly, the rise in affluence was accompanied by growth in consumption. Individual consumption rose, as evidenced in the growing rate of expenditures from personal incomes, which increased at the record rate of 8.3% in 1996 (relative to the previous year), by 6.9% in 1997, and by 6.4%. in 1999. According to analysts, such as Robert Skidelsky (1999), and economic practitioners, such as Jeffrey Sachs (1993), Poland became a leader in the changes which cleared the way for capitalism, with Poland's indexes of economic advancement surpassing those of the Czech Republic, Hungary and other post-communist nations going through shock therapy.

In most general terms, these findings are reflected in the dynamics of the aggregate index of wellbeing provided by GDP per capita. While in 1990, GDP per capita in Poland was $1,547, by 1999 it had more than doubled, reaching $3,702. The figures are surprisingly impressive when compared with the GDP dynamics in Norway, Switzerland and the United States, the leading economies of the time. Over those nine years, their advantage over Poland decreased by half. In 1990, GDP per capita in Switzerland was 21.7 times as high as that in Poland ($33,600 and $1,500, respectively), but already in 1999 it was only 9.6 times as high as in Poland. The corresponding figures for Norway and the United States dropped from 17.6 to 9.5 and from 14.6 to 7.9, respectively, in favour of Poland. Apparently, Poland was quite efficient in closing the gap in the pursuit of middle-class societies.

Data from the national surveys conducted in 1987 and 1998 show how these processes unfolded in terms of material possessions. The findings reveal a significant increase in possession of cars, washing machines, video cameras, computers, TV sets and other commodities. While in 1987 merely 29% of families owned a colour TV set, eleven years later more than 90% could afford one. In 1998, 33% of families had cable television, and 19% satellite television. Computers were a new addition to the household equipment. The percentage of computer owners picked up from 1% to 14%, and of video camera owners from 2% to 7%. In the 1980s there were no cell phones, which are now common belongings among all social categories. In 1998, automatic washing machines were owned by 69% of families, refrigerators by 97% and cars by 53%. In the case of cars, the proportion nearly doubled as compared to 27% in 1987 (Domański 2000a). The 638,000 new cars sold in 1999 saw Poland move to third place on the European automobile market.

These developmental tendencies were boosted first of all by higher incomes, consumption needs swelling when consumption appeared affordable and an eagerness to compensate for years upon years of dearth and sacrifices. "Macro-economic stabilisation" and "structural adjustment" became favourite economic bywords, which in colloquial translation meant more or less "curbing inflation" and "cutting down on subsidies for loss-generating firms." Poland managed to stop the printing of empty money, reduce the budget deficit and make sure that zloty exchange rates remained realistic. The country failed, however, to complete priva-tisation and the restructuring of non-profitable industries. What later came to be called shock therapy was not just a single exploit of price release and currency sta-bilisation, but a several-year-long project implemented by Tadeusz Mazowiecki's cabinet, who certainly took heed of Machiavelli's advice to start from the most difficult decisions and then reap the fruits which would gradually follow.

In formulating a tentative assessment of these changes, one can usefully learn from comparisons with Western societies. Their prosperity commenced in the era of post-war reconstruction, the Marshall plan and an economic boom. At that time, Poland was going through intensive industrialisation. In all likelihood, it will be a considerable challenge to approximate the material standard of liv-ing of the West after several decades of enforced stagnation. It will take time to modernise the economy and dismantle traditional habits. The standard of living, however, has undeniably improved. After 50 years of communism, an average citizen finally has a chance to relish more quotidian achievements than peaking figures of pig iron and steam locomotive production.

Style

Genuine shock therapies redraw attitudes and refashion life styles. Given this, two reservations should be made which bid caution in envisioning a robust rise of the Polish middle class. Firstly, an improvement in material prosperity does not automatically result in respective changes of attitudes and values. Secondly, what is customarily identified as a typical middle-class life style spreads mainly among people who aspire to progress and have promotion opportunities. Disseminating middle-class patterns poses challenges comparable to the difficulties occasioned by searching for a common language for groups of higher and lower social statuses. Joining an elite group requires good recommendations, a proper appearance and natural manners, and likewise, for a middle-class society to arise certain conditions must be met in a sustained process in which its would-be members must overcome a series of mental obstacles.

The middle-class style is likely to take a few generations to develop in Poland, though things now look admittedly more promising than, say, a hundred years ago. In Edwardian England, everyone's status could be recognised from 200 yards away – according to Orwell (1961), a gentleman was identified by his dress and gestures. Later experience of British society with the Labour Party governments made such assessments remote. In Poland, class divisions became obliterated by the wholesale policy of egalitarianism enforced by the communist regime. We are, however, interested less in the gentleman vs. the working class distinction and more in the middle-class style as a macro-level characteristic of Polish society. The scope of changes and the scale of progress are difficult to assess with any precision because under the former regime no studies examined the middle class and, consequently, we are unable to establish "point zero," that is, the situation from before the political shift. What we can offer is an account of the current condition, which may provide grounds for reflection on how far the life style patterns of market societies have made inroads into Poland.

Enter a man's home and you will identify his class at first sight. When applied to empirical research, it means that the conditions in which people live their private lives are particularly reliable indicators of their social position. By the 1990s, three quarters of British citizens lived in their own homes (notably, 50% of workers owned a house) – a figure unmatched by any other country. Fond of visual effects, worker families furnish their house facades with ample lighting, place plastic gnomes in front lawns and have their stuccowork-embellished lamps exposed for everybody to admire. Lower middle-class homes resound with selected pieces of classical music (an important indication of commitment to high culture), while Queen and the likes of it are played in worker-inhabited houses. Undoubtedly, owning a house testifies to opportunities for and aspirations to higher status. Also in Poland, more and more young married couples from the intelligentsia or business backgrounds purchase a house at the very start of their new life.

A house alone does not suffice, however. With residential segregation in place, middle class membership requires also an "appropriate" address because geographical divisions of towns overlap with class barriers. Area of residence has been taken into account since the onset of research on social stratification. In American "community studies," the residential area was found to be one of the four components of the Index of Status Characteristics constructed by L.W. Warner, alongside occupational position, source and size of incomes (Warner 1949). The pioneering study of the English middle class in Bethnal Green reported that 90% of all the working class members who had been born there never left the place, living next door to families and close kin (Young and Willmott 1957). Each town has its better and worse neighbourhoods. The former, enjoying prestige, better housing facilities and well maintained streets, are inhabited by the social categories which occupy the higher rungs of the social ladder. The residents of better-off neighbourhoods occasionally campaign against erecting worker estates in their vicinity in order to avoid unwelcome misidentification.

Similar tendencies are on the rise in Poland. For example, Warsaw's suburb of Międzylesie has become a coveted retreat for the capital's wealthiest residents. In 2000, home sites there sold at $30-60 per square metre. However, there is still another suburb, Konstancin, which enjoys the unparalleled repute of being the most prestigious residential area, with the elites unanimously proclaiming that "if you do not live in Konstancin, you are a non-entity in Warsaw's salons." In the communist period, the intelligentsia had lived next door to plumbers and tailors for decades. At present, however, a process is suddenly unfolding which seems explicable only by the impact of the symbiotic need to dwell in the company of peers. The smell of Sunday roast enveloping the staircase, once a familiar element of the local colour, comes across as irritatingly coarse now. For those who can afford considerable spendings, newly built estates are advertised as the dream of security, comfort and recreation come true – apparent oases of privacy. Other assets guaranteed in the advertising leaflets include tennis courts, playgrounds and barbecue venues in the vicinity, as well as security services round the clock. For the new intelligentsia, a house is about to become a genuine haven. In 2001, the average apartment price in Warsaw and its surroundings stood at $500-620 per 1 square metre, but for the most expensive exclusive apartments in Śródmieście it neared $2,500 ("Rest assured, to buy a house you won't have to crack your favourite money box."). And the demand for elegant luxury residences does not seem to subside.

Real estate owners are the axis of the middle class. Having bought an apartment or a house, a citizen becomes a more credible partner for the government, the police, banks and all those who respect the law and appreciate the charms of quiet life. Ownership breeds trust and secures better treatment for the residents of affluent neighbourhoods; banks, for one, are more willing (eager even) to give loans to them than to the members of declining housing cooperatives – pensioners, retirees and public-sector employees.

Senior managers and specialists know how to spend their time better than the lower classes. Information about patterns of spending leisure time is supplied by research from the 1990s. In a nationwide survey carried out in 1998, the respondents were asked: "Some people engage in certain activities relatively often, others sometimes, still others very seldom, and some never at all. Specify, please, how often you do the following…" Here followed a list of 20 activities, including "activity for a party or a political association," "activity for a trade union," "engaging in services for the local community," "watching TV," "hanging around the house, looking out of the window, talking with neighbours," "eating out or going to a club," "doing crossword puzzles," and "sewing or knitting." The respondents indicated which of those they did "very often," "quite often," "rather rarely," and "very rarely or never" (Domański 2000a).

Watching TV was decisively the most frequently chosen item. Forty-one percent of the respondents reported that they "very often" spent their time in front of the television. Other activities involved DIY, including "mending something round the house" (29%), family visits (19%) and "a hobby" pursued by 12% of the representatives of the adult population. Only 2% of the respondents declared that they "often" "surveyed stock exchange quotations," and 5% chose "activity in professional associations," both associated with professionalisation based on healthy capitalist principles and business logic. As can be easily guessed, "dealing with the stock exchange" was most frequently picked by company directors (14%) and "activity in professional associations" by the intelligentsia (13%), but across the other categories the popularity of these pursuits was relatively scarce.

One reason for eating out instead of at home is to add some variety to the daily routine and satisfy a need for luxury. Results from the 1998 survey revealed that 8.5% of adult Poles went out for lunch or dinner – specifically, the 8.5% refers to the respondents declaring that they ate out at least "a few times a year" in response to the question: "Do you meet up with your acquaintances at restaurants?" The category consisted mostly of the intelligentsia (18.5%–18.6%) and, in a lesser degree, of business owners, executives, and, in general, senior managerial staff and administrative officials. For some of them, eating out might have been an attractive way to enact aspirations of being waited on in non-standard circumstances, while for others in might have represented a coveted luxury. The intelligentsia went to restaurants twice as often as skilled workers. Eating out epitomises a typically urban style, which seemed rather alien to did not apply to farmers.

Eating out for business is an even more conspicuous symbol of modernity associated with the middle class. All in all, 3.8% of the respondents stated that they would eat a business lunch "a few times a year." The restaurant turned out the relatively most often chosen meeting venue for senior managerial staff and the non-technical intelligentsia (authors, artists, marketing specialists, scholars, doctors and lawyers) – 14–15% of them attended business lunches. Business owners scored third (12.2%), and the technical intelligentsia (engineers) fourth (9.4%). Eating out for business hardly applied to manual workers and peasants. Eating in restaurants is not only a business duty or a strategy for success in negotiations. It also becomes a pleasure and increases social prestige.

Analysing health-related life styles, Antonina Ostrowska (1997) reported that a pro-healthy style prevailed in the categories at the higher rungs of social stratification. People who approach life with thoughtful responsibility and have long-term orientations do sports and see a dentist regularly. Rational individuals invest in health, which they view as a form of capital, in keeping with Henry Ford's recommendations of hard work: one needs health to attain a high social position, get promoted and earn decent money. This teaching falls on fertile soil in Poland, though we still lag behind the Western standards. For now, the most encouraging symptoms of change have been observed in the structure of food consumption. In 1995, the consumption of beef (a risk factor in increasing circulatory hazards) dropped to 53.4% of the 1989 level. With beef being gradually abandoned, Poles started to eat more poultry and fish; consumption of poultry grew in particular (by 21.4%) according to the statistics of the Food and Nutrition Institute (Instytut Żywności i Żywienia). In the corresponding period, consumption of vegetable fat increased by 163.6%, consumption of animal fat dropped, and more fruit and more vegetables were eaten in Poland.

Not much is known about other changes in pro-healthy life styles. A study conducted in 1998 concluded that 34.7% of Poles had a dental check-up at least once a year, and 34.4% signed up for periodic medical examinations (including blood analysis, ECG or an X-ray) of their own accord, but only 4.6% "drank juices and ate fresh fruit" (Domański 2000b). The life style of Poles is closer to that of the "lower class" with their preference for stodgy meals and canned food. On the whole, a disregard of the rules of healthy nutrition is one of our serious weaknesses.

Only with the coming of middle-class societies did sports win general appreciation. Sports became pleasure and relaxation after a day's work, as well as, for the heirs of the Protestant ethics, a surrogate of success in leisure time. The politically turbulent history of the People's Republic of Poland knew several moments of (governmentally authorised) "opening up" to Western sports. Another such opening came in the 1990s when jogging aficionados and amateur cyclists took to the streets. As some sports rise and some fall in prestige, new status symbols keep emerging. The surfboard is ousting the tennis racket.

In the 1998 survey, the respondents answered whether "they practice sports in their free time." The enclosed list included 11 sports disciplines. Amateurs of sports recreation were in the minority: 21.9% of the people surveyed stated that they had no time for sports, and another 32.8% declared that they "don't need to practice sports." Among those respondents who did a sport, 3.7% played tennis in their free time, 4.2% skied, and 10.7% jogged. The relatively most elitist disciplines included golf (0.3%), surfing (0.4%), sailing (1.6%) and horseback-riding (1.6%). Those were pursued most often by business owners, far more rarely by the non-technical intelligentsia, and rarer still by technicians, mid-ranked administrative staff and sales and services workers. The rule that a lower occupational position is a weaker incentive for engaging in more stimulating sports seems to hold also in Poland. Such sports remain the domain of high-status individuals who habitually think in profit-and-loss categories, or the nouveau-riches, who can afford the costs incurred in practicing them.

It is June 2002. If we ask whether we are anywhere near middle-class society, we must in all honesty respond that we are not, not really. But we are nearer that point than the English were in the early 1950s. In the first half of the 1950s, the UK experienced a transition from the post-war privation times to the "opulence" era. Below, an excerpt form David Lodge's autobiographical novel *Out of the Shelter* recapitulates the problems a typical English family coped with in those days: "I don't know what Christmas would be without you, Kath, his father said. There's nothing in the shops. Rationing's terrible – worse than the war, said his mother. Bread's the latest, if you don't mind. – I don't understand it, said Kath. You seem to be no better off than the Germans [...]. Despite all the presents that Kath had brought, it wasn't a very merry Christmas. There was a power-cut on Christmas Day which spoiled the dinner. Kath kept complaining of the cold, but they didn't have much cal and his parents kept bickering about the fire" (1989: 37–38). The English economy overcame the post-war slump relatively quickly. In Poland, too, the rationing system and shortage economy are things of the past and unlikely to return.

What Could Not Happen in the USA:
Controversies around Enfranchisement

In terms of affluence, Polish society has made undeniable progress. Certain indicators of prosperity, especially cars, apartments and houses, induce a sense of having fate under control, even if some of these goods are in fact owned by a bank and it will take dozens of years of uncertainty to pay the loans off. But this is exactly how the middle class phenomenon works psychologically – it enforces rational behaviours and self-discipline, providing incentives which facilitate coping with difficulties. In Western societies, the middle class embodies advancement, marshals criteria for individuals' social utility and stimulates exertions for the sake of self-development. For those who identify with it, the middle class is a standard of unquestioned validity. And for the capitalist system, it is a guarantee of stability and effectiveness.

And indeed, the middle class is essentially a normative model of society to strive for. As Alexis de Tocqueville (1954 ed.) explained in the 19th century in the chapter "Why the Americans are so restless in the midst of their prosperity" of his *Democracy in America*, the Americans know no peace until they contrive to obtain the most rewarding occupational position, find proper lodgings and ensure the most advantageous living conditions, that is, achieve a certainty that they have done their absolute best. They find satisfaction in that exploit for a fleeting moment only to wish for more still as soon as their previous promptings are gratified. If transported to today's Poland, de Tocqueville, though a very insightful observer, would be hard pressed to detect signs of the creative ferment which makes people endowed with free will push forward and abhor stopping half-way. The most energetic individuals swarm in advertising, banking and marketing – a narrow sector of profit-focused modern enterprises.

Optimistic findings were reported in the research conducted by Aleksander Marcinkowski (1996) among Cracow's businessmen. In his study he identified a "restless spirit" syndrome, manifesting in high occupational mobility among his respondents-entrepreneurs, most of whom had worked in many companies and firms and done internships abroad (47% of the sample). The average citizen is still only learning the rules of the game, but the fact that 2% of the population own shares in quoted companies and another 2% are unitholders in investment funds (according to the Public Opinion Research Centre [CBOS] 1999 surveys) is certainly not the worst of harbingers. It must be remembered that bank deposits warrant greater security and less risk, and risk was deemed a vice in the classical "spirit of capitalism" norms.

The point which Poland has reached on the developmental trajectory of middle-class society is open to various assessments. One of the applicable frameworks of reference is provided by Max Lerner's (1961) typology of the American middle class based on individual strategies for life. The typology includes a category of "neutral technicians," i.e. disciplined employees who comply with the expectations for a man of success as envisioned by the middle class. Nevertheless, as Lerner argues, neutral technicians observe the hallowed norms of "the middle classes" as a result of coercion exercised by the structures, which leave individuals no other choice. Neutral technicians fundamentally differ from resourceful individualists and nearly merge with "conformists," who stray even further away from the classical ethos of the enterprising individual.

This seems to be the case of small and medium-sized company owners in Poland. According to Juliusz Gardawski's 1998 research (2001), company owners found it easier to make routine decisions concerning their familiar market niche than to develop into marketing experts who closely scrutinise economic trends and react accordingly, depending on the fluctuating circumstances. In all likelihood, the commitment to "cultivating one's own garden" will not subside or recede any time soon. This, however, is no reason for shame, because all middle-class societies seem to remain children of necessity from the perspective of their average members.

Nobody is perfect. Even the greatest champions of the middle class are not exempt from unlooked-for blunders. In 2000, after a heated public debate featuring conflicting arguments advanced by the various parties involved, the Polish Parliament passed an enfranchisement bill. The bill stipulated that ownership of co-operative and company flats would be transferred to their tenants at a token price of 3% of their market value. Reputed economic experts and scholars, largely appreciative of the middle class, lashed out with scathing critique. In berating the bill's provisions, they argued that the tenants were altogether unprepared to be owners because they had neither the financial resources nor the sufficient capabilities to take good care of the property gifted them by the state. Proclamations of this kind would be utterly unimaginable in the United States. Middle-class interests are traditionally the main object of the promises made by American politicians, and "the middle class" is mulled over and over again in annual presidential addresses to the nation. Any public expression of doubt as to whether society identified with the middle class is ready to take the helm of their lives would be tantamount to negating the very core of market democracy, and thus entail political suicide. All of which actually does not mean that in the case of Poland such doubts are unfounded.

Chapter III: Self-Reliance: 1984–1998

> *Seat thyself sultanically among the moons of Saturn, and take high abstracted man alone; and he seems a wonder, a grandeur, and a woe. But from that same point, take mankind in mass, and for the most part, they seem a mob of unnecessary duplicates...*

> Herman Melville, *Moby Dick*

Individualistic orientations have become a signature token of Western societies confident in the power of success and espousing a realistic approach to life models. In a very basic sense, individualism is expressed in an agentive capacity to determine one's career. In the wake of the dissolution of the feudal estate system, the triumph of individualism was first beaconed when outstanding commoners could simply ignore the unwanted presence of the upper-class members. In the political and occupational spheres, individualism found support in universal suffrage and the ideology of equal opportunity. If in the feudal system individualism could only be a high-minded call to respect individual rights advocated by the theorists of the social contract, after the dismantling of estate barriers, it could indeed materialise in practice.

Individualism was furnished with ideological justifications by economic liberalism and philosophical utilitarianism. A religious thrust was provided by Protestant ethics – Jean Calvin's merits in this respect equal those of Jeremy Bentham, a founder of utilitarianism, and Adam Smith, the father of classical economy, in their respective domains. All three of them were fervent supporters of individualism and espoused the credo of giving everybody maximum freedom to pursue their life goals and show their mettle. Only in this way can it be ascertained whether one has risen to the challenge of destiny and what one is really capable of. The principles were put into effect – the burden of self-reliance was shouldered by enfranchised peasants, and workers, who had shuffled off the constraints of the guild system, were basically left no other option. The most spectacular exploits, however, belonged to the middle classes, which engaged in rivalry at work in order to prove both to themselves and to others that they mattered as individuals.

Individual success became a major constituent of an overall life career. The European newcomers who settled New England in the 17th century extolled an entrepreneurial penchant as a special virtue. With occupational positions no longer inherited, building a successful company from scratch or steadily climbing up the promotion ladder was a particularly appreciated demonstration of capacity and perseverance. American Sunday schools idolised Abraham Lincoln, who was revered first of all for his prudence, drive for knowledge, outstanding ambition and single-handedly attained success. Edified by faith and examples of the authentic fortunes made before their eyes, members of the middle class confidently headed into life.

What does individual success mean today? While for some it still remains a heartening legend and a goal to accomplish, for others it connotes a threat. De Tocqueville (1954 ed.) praised it for stimulating people's constructive involvements and fostering democratic values (in America "no natural boundary seems to be set to the efforts of man") but insisted that there was only a thin line between individualism and "savagery." For many decades to come, the hearty endorsement of individualism was intertwined with a sharp criticism of it. Exponents of disparate worldviews, theoretical frameworks and political allegiances, such as Lerner (1961), Mills (1965), Riesman (1971), Lasch (1982), Gans (1988), Donohue (1990), Dore (1992), Etzioni (1994) and Derber (1996), have all been particularly eager to denounce the destructive implications of the drive for self-reliance, which, if excessive, destabilises individuals' minds and threatens to destroy social bonds and communal sentiments. The most scathing critique is habitually showered on self-centredness and egoism as inherent in individualism. Such accusations were poignantly articulated in Tom Wolfe's famous article "The 'me' decade and the third awakening," which appeared in the September 1976 issue of the *New York Times Magazine*. The eponymous "me" designated pathological self-absorption. In Wolfe's account, the young Americans who were discussed in the article had become heartless egoists, and the 70s were a morally depraved epoch in which the generally more altruistic climate of the 1960s had all but dissipated.

Individualism faced a threat in the 1930s, when the liberal economic doctrine found itself under attack and the capitalist economy plummeted. Huge public works programmes were used extensively in both Franklin Delano Roosevelt's and Nazi Germany's policies for staving off the meltdown, with the American notion of *boondoggles*, i.e. pointless projects, echoed in the German *Pyrammidenbau*. Roosevelt's Brain Trust members – such as Rex Tugwell and Adolf Berle (a co-author with Means of *The Modern Corporation*, published in 1932, where the impending "managerial revolution" is prophesied) – advocated setting up policy-planning offices for every production branch. In its 1941 vision of post-war life, the British Labour Party trumpeted a social welfare state assuming responsibility for the lives of the citizens and making sure they were secure till the end of their days.

Although in the aftermath of the war the process of re-installing liberal capitalism commenced, liberalisation experienced also a few relapses. A major setback took place in the 1970s. Responding to growing poverty rates and pressure from trade unions, most Western governments undertook to combat "social problems" by instituting "social wages," pro-unionist legislation and workplace protection laws. Such policies ebbed in the 1980s, when the joint efforts of Margaret Thatcher and Ronald Reagan in ideologically inspiring and fuelling the fight against collectivism produced fertile ground for the revival of individualistic orientations. Born into an Irish immigrant family in a small Midwestern town, Reagan was raised to believe in individual self-determination. Thatcher, in turn, was a disciple of Hayek, and the seed sown by the author of *The Road to Serfdom* came to fruition when the Conservatives stepped into power. Thatcher's views on the role of the state are pithily encapsulated in her autobiography: "It was the job of government to establish a framework of stability […] We had to get out of the business of telling people what their ambitions should be and how exactly to realize them" (Thatcher 1993: pp. 14–15). Individualism turned into a doctrine capable of lifting the frustration of a society disaffected with technocratic regulations and trade-union corporatism.

With the promotion of individual achievement, less attention is paid to the individual's class membership, group affiliations or bonds with the state, the nation and the party. The idea of individualism could not but find a natural enemy in societies of real socialism, where the collective interest was a supreme value vastly overriding individuals' uncontrolled, robust activity, which only threatened to disperse energy and incur losses. Whereas under the socialist system individualism was antithetical to the centrally planned economy and social life, it should have become a pronounced influence in social relationships in contemporary Poland, corresponding to the nature and the scale of the transformations at hand. Has it put down roots yet? This question signals three issues for us to address.

The first issue is how individualistic attitudes have developed over time. To expect too much would be unreasonable because a disposition for self-reliance depends largely on personality and is not easily amenable to external pressures. However, there is no denying that the institutional constraints imposed upon enterprising people by the former regime have already eroded to the point of non-existence. The logic of capitalist rationality has ousted the spirit of collectivism from companies, which have stopped supplying employees with provisions, organising holidays and allocating flats. Pro-active attitudes are encouraged by a diversity of available consumer goods, but they received a truly decisive thrust from the liberalisation of ownership restrictions. The desire to possess outpaces collective allegiances when people start to work for themselves and in their own businesses. In the ideology of capitalist free competition, setting up a business ushered one into the antechamber of success: a worker was first to become a foreman and then an industrialist, a clerk was to turn independent tradesman, and a peasant's son was to develop into a landholding farmer. In Poland in the 1990s, the opponents of collectivist modes paired the orientation of success with ownership, but whether this has been followed by a change in mentality and is discernible in everyday conduct remains yet to be seen. The question arises of how far a self-reliant individual capable of making choices and handling life pressures has become a familiar figure among Poles.

The second issue to be considered is where in the social hierarchy individualistic attitudes are anchored. Research conducted after the systemic breakthrough implies that such attitudes are concentrated in three major segments which possess property in a broad sense of the term: business people, who own companies; the intelligentsia, who have higher education; and senior managers, who possess what the intelligentsia have and additionally the organisational capital, a capacity for its practical application and power (Domański and Dukaczewska 1997). Theoretically, these three categories should be the recipients of the financial profits and prestige brought about by capitalism, and thus be best equipped to cultivate self-centred attitudes. Admittedly, this is by far the simplest version of the story, which is not necessarily an accurate one.

The third issue to investigate is how diversified the inclinations toward self-reliance are. Again, arguably, the differences should prove larger after the systemic change. Conditions particularly conducive to individualism have emerged at the top rung of the occupational ladder where previously unknown occupations have appeared, such as consultants, investment advisers, stock brokers, marketing experts and public relations specialists. A degree, be it even a degree from a prestigious university, is not necessarily a guarantee of a good job. Companies have varied requirements for employment, but they all tend to give precedence to skills over formal educational credentials. "I appreciate it when a candidate defines his occupational ambitions precisely," states a consultant at Neumann Int. in an interview for *Rzeczpospolita* (one of Poland's leading dailies) (2000), "it shows where he is headed in life. Another thing I pay attention to are his career achievements. What I mean is working on particular projects, for example restructuring a company, taking it public, or developing a marketing strategy." Used by relatively few people yet, the Internet is a truly elitist medium on the labour market in Poland. Recruiters for electronic trading companies seek first of all energetic, talented and passionate candidates. Similarly, training specialists in on-line commerce underscore that a premium is put on particular personal endowments: successful candidates are competent, independent and goal-oriented. Employers seek, first of all, "life entrepreneurs" and visionaries.

At the same time, the risk of unemployment is spreading. The CBOS surveys (1998) reveal that in 1998 46% of the population feared that their company might be closed down or their farm/business might go bankrupt, and 36% did not think their jobs were secure. Three years later, in a survey carried out by the CBOS in August 2001, 41% of the adult Poles sampled reported that they felt at risk of redundancy. When no company is deemed a secure workplace, long-term thinking grows in importance. If the valuable capitals of ownership have spurred aspirations for self-determination, at the opposite pole a mentality has burgeoned which counts on the state and social welfare. Representatives of the working class do not have marketable capitals at their disposal, and an awareness of limited acquisitive opportunities combined with low incomes saps their motivation for seeking status. The capitalist logic impairs those groups which have little to offer employers and society (the author intentionally uses the parlance of the enlightened elites, among whom a "lack of something to offer" is a favourite codeword). This is the main reason why the vision of a neat, hedgerow-encircled house does not particularly hold sway over the lower classes.

In Poland, the major assets of the industrial working class are the trade unions, mass demonstrations and group solidarity. These capitals prompt a rather different sort of activity than professional qualifications, a business or expertise do. What meanings does the collective protest of the lower classes have? Certainly, it signifies more than a mere herding instinct. And since ambivalence pervades most behaviours, falling back on collectivist strategies does not preclude searching for individual paths to success. For a few decades now, scholars have studied the so-called instrumental collectivism of the working class in Western societies. Instrumental collectivism, which is used to describe efforts geared to realise individual selfish interest through organised action, was examined thoroughly in *The Affluent Worker* (1969). According to the study's four authors – British researchers Goldthorpe, Lockwood, Platt and Bechhoffer – instrumental collectivism, on the side of assets, produces a sense of power, facilitates satisfaction of claims and strengthens self-worth in the lower classes. As such, in Poland it could be a remedy of sorts for the intellectual aloofness and superciliousness of the elites. Such attitudes have been shown to be a durable feature of the British working class (Parkin 1979, Marshall et al. 1988, Marshall 1997). Notably, in terms of satisfaction of group interests, instrumental collectivism of the working class corresponds to analogous strategies practised by corporations of medical doctors, lawyers and engineers, who embody the classical individualism of the new middle-class variety.

Individualistic orientations are multidimensional and related to various developments. Because the most important breakthrough in this respect was provided by the systemic changes of 1989, the issues signalled above can be explored only by recourse to data which cover a time span. Drawing on the findings from studies carried out in 1984, 1995 and 1998 on representative Polish adult samples, I have compared certain aspects of individualistic orientations as captured in the late 1990s and in the preceding decade. In all those surveys, the respondents answered analogous questions, serving to identify those attitudes characteristic of self-reliance, that is, an attribute which Mills (1965) identified as emblematic of the American middle classes.[1] A comparison of self-reliance levels observed in 1984, 1995 and 1998 allows us to establish three points. Firstly, whether the desire for self-reliance grew, declined or, perhaps, remained unchanged in the wake of the abolition of the centralised management of public life – a lack of change cannot be ruled out since individualism is a personality trait, basically immune to external changes. Secondly, how the dynamics of such attitudes developed in the middle class to be, that is, in the intelligentsia, managerial staff and business people. And thirdly, whether alongside the development of the market economy individualistic attitudes became a more relevant dimension of the social

---

1   The 1998 study was carried out on a random, nationwide representative sample of adult Poles (over 18 years). The effective sample based on individual addresses included 1,596 respondents, both male and female. The survey was part of my grant project funded by the KBN [the State Committee for Scientific Research] (1 HO1F 012 13). The research team included faculty of the Institute of Philosophy and Sociology at the Polish Academy of Sciences: H. Domański, F. Sztabiński, P. Sztabiński and W. Wesołowski. The 1995 study was carried out by a team including most researchers of the sociology division of the Institute of Philosophy and Sociology at the Polish Academy of Sciences. The survey included a random address-based sample of Poles aged 18-70 (see Domański et al. 1997). The 1984 study was carried out on a national sample of 1,911 respondents (based on combined quota- and random sampling) within a research project headed by W. Adamski. Sampling and representativeness details are explained elsewhere (see Domański 1986).

hierarchy, that is, whether in the 1990s they were a stronger differentiating factor than before.

Individualism on a Decline

The data from Table 2 imply certain conclusions about how Poles' aspirations for self-reliance changed between 1984 and 1998. The respondents were asked to assess four items on a four-point scale. The items were: (i) I have little influence over the things that happen to me, (ii) I believe that what is going to happen will happen, (iii) if I fail, it is not my fault in most cases, (iv) most of my problems are usually a matter of bad luck or adverse circumstances. The possible responses (on four-points scales) were: "I definitely agree," "I rather agree," "I rather disagree," "I definitely disagree." My point is to establish how the summary responses to the four items compare.

Table 2: Distribution of respondents across the self-reliance scale in 1984, 1995 and 1998 (in %)

Self-reliance scale	Percentage		
	1984	1995	1998
1–4	2.7	2.5	2.7
5–8	21.0	41.8	30.0
9–12	69.8	53.8	58.9
13–16	6.5	1.9	8.4
Total	100.0	100.0	100.0
Mean	10.4	9.0	9.5

Factor analysis showed that both in 1984 and in the later years, the responses formed one dimension. Thus, the response "I definitely disagree" in any of the items was connected with "I definitely disagree" in the remaining three items. Such responses were provided by individuals who were the most determined to rely on themselves for overcoming obstacles in life. People with the least inclination to face up to adversity ("I definitely agree") were situated on the opposite pole.[2]

The items come from a questionnaire used in research on the personality trait which psychologists refer to as "the locus of control" (Rotter 1966). Out of the original set of eight items, I selected the four presented above, which turned out

---

2   The "factor" they formed in 1984 "explained" 27.4% of the variation between all items; the corresponding value in 1998 stood at 25.3%.

to make the dominant axis along which attitudes varied, ranging from assuming full responsibility for oneself to passivity and fatalism. The subjects responded to each item using scores from 1 to 4. The four scores were added to render an aggregate score on the self-reliance scale, ranging from the lowest of 4 to the theoretical maximum of 16, which provided a summary index of the intensity of self-reliant attitudes. The bottom row of Table 2 presents the mean levels of such attitudes in 1984, 1995 and 1998, and the upper rows show proportions of the respondents in particular brackets of the self-reliance scale. Comparing these findings, we may establish whether any upward or downward shifts took place over the 14 years.

The declared level of individualism did not grow and even declined a little, if we regard a certain drop in the mean score as significant. In 1984, the mean stood at 10.4 points, in 1995 at 9 points, and in 1998 at 9.5 points. Given the undoubtedly slight, but noteworthy decrease, we may legitimately conclude that the consolidation of the market economy did not trigger widespread individualistic orientations. The capitalist market mechanisms failed to incite Poles to take initiative and assume responsibility for their lives, or at least if such decisions were indeed made, they were not voluntary choices. In 1998, people with self-declared individualism scores below the mid-point of the scale accounted for 32.7% of the entire sample while in 1984 for only 23.7%. At the same time, however, the percentage of the respondents with the relatively highest individualism scores picked up from 6.5% to 8.4%.

What can be inferred from these figures? Contrary to expectations, the spread of the market economy apparently did not encourage greater self-reliance in Poles. Under communism, a common conviction was that society yearned for the barriers to individualism to be lifted and would reveal its true character as soon as those obstacles were removed. Since the early 1990s, private enterprises have proliferated and, as I attempted to show in the foregoing, educational capital now translates into higher income. The market mechanisms, however, have not enhanced the readiness to take risk. Perhaps, contrary to what used to be our reputation, we are not a nation of individualists after all. People simply do not seem to realise that they should rely on themselves more than before. The message of self-sufficiency has failed to trickle down despite the advances of capitalism, the growing meritocracy and greater opportunities to utilise individual "capitals," all of which afford more chances to the ambitious and the talented.

Has Self-Reliance Become a More Important Dimension of the Social Hierarchy?

A decrease in the mean level of individualistic attitudes may imply that they have become a less relevant factor in social stratification. However, the lack of a growth tendency was revealed only on the general national level, and it need not hold true for all Poles. Among them, we should focus particularly on the intelligentsia, higher managerial staff and owners of businesses, that is, the categories which are the greatest beneficiaries of the expanding market economy and exhibited the greatest individualistic orientations in the early 1990s (Domański and Dukaczewska 1997). These observations need to be confirmed especially since the data in Table 2 suggest that the category reporting the most pronounced individualistic orientations is growing. We must ask, specifically, whether a proclivity for self-reliance has become a factor which, alongside other ones, makes social stratification more rigid.

To establish that, I used a simple criterion: a preference for self-reliance becomes a more significant dimension of social stratification if it differentiates Polish society more strongly. This can happen also when individualistic orientations are almost the same on the national level, as was the case in the 1980-90s.

Table 3: Self-reliance in socio-occupational categories and in socio-occupational categories of fathers. Mean values for the self-reliance scale in 1984 and 1998

Socio-occupational categories	Self-reliance			
	Respondents		Respondents' fathers	
	1984	1998	1984	1998
Higher managerial staff and administrative officials	11.8	11.2	11.6	10.5
Non-technical intelligentsia	11.6	10.5	11.4	10.8
Technical intelligentsia	11.2	10.9	11.2	10.8
Technicians	10.9	9.6	10.7	10.4
Mid-ranked administrative staff	10.7	10.3	11.0	10.3
Clerical workers	10.0	9.7	10.9	11.1
Owners	11.1	10.5	9.9	9.8
Sales and services	10.5	9.5	10.3	9.7
Foremen	9.8	10.0	10.2	9.2
Skilled workers	10.1	9.3	10.3	9.8
Unskilled workers in production	9.7	8.8	10.5	8.7
Unskilled workers in services	9.2	8.7	11.2	9.3
Agricultural workers	10.3	8.3	9.7	9.2
Farm owners	10.0	8.6	10.1	8.9
Mean	10.4	9.5	10.3	9.5
Correlation ratio	0.23	0.27	0.15	0.26

The first two columns of Table 3 contain mean scores on the self-reliance scale in 1984 and 1998 for the basic categories of social stratification. Let us start with comparing the values of the correlation ratio, which show how strongly membership in those categories was related to declared self-reliance. Between 1984 and 1998 the values of this measure rose from 0.23 to 0.27. This might suggest that differences among the categories became more pronounced. However, the distances between the categories were relatively minor. The greatest sense of individualism was reported by senior executives. In 1984, the distance between them and the bottom group on the self-reliance scale, that is, manual workers in services (e.g. janitors, paramedics or cleaners) amounted to 2.6 points. In the 1990s, agricultural workers dropped to the lowest position, scoring 2.9 points less than upper managerial staff in 1998. Importantly, agricultural workers, most of them former employees of state-owned collective farms now hired by individual farmers, have experienced social degradation across the spectrum of inequality. Having lost the guaranteed stable employment, tolerable standard of living and social security they had enjoyed under the previous regime, agricultural workers represent classic sufferers of economic privation due to the shrinkage of social welfare.

The relatively lowest level of individualist attitudes in agricultural workers reflects the logic which underpins the on-going transformation. It might reveal a latent, passive servant-mentality permeated by deference for authority and social seniors, which has been found among British agricultural workers. This attitude involves acceptance of one's own very low status combined with overt admiration towards supervisors. The stance of lowly humbleness observed in British farm workers was unheard-of in British democracy. The authors of the study interpreted the findings as expressive of attachment to patriarchy and a reminiscence of esteem shown to the upper ranks in estate societies, where a vassal's prostration went hand in hand with a serf's subservience (Newby 1977).

In Poland, symptoms of a decreasing proclivity for self-reliance were reported for all categories except foremen. Foremen, i.e. supervisory workers, reported higher individualism scores in 1998 than in the 1980s (although this could have only been an ostensible rise, related to a small number of foremen; consequently, the mean figures may fail to reflect the actual tendencies). The biggest drop in inclinations toward self-reliance was registered in agricultural workers, the intelligentsia and peasants. Despite that, the intelligentsia still scored relatively high and shared top standings with senior managers and owners. Because downward tendencies affected all categories rather evenly without causing fundamental displacements, the stratification of these attitudes remained stable, overlapping with the classical ladders of income, prestige and power.

The intelligentsia and senior managers are followed by mid-ranked administrative staff, with workers and farmers trailing behind with the lowest reported levels of self-reliance. Arguably, in the case of peasants, habits ingrained by a family-based, traditionally patriarchal community clash with the individualistic orientations of ownership. In countries with a high proportion of peasantry, Poland being one such, social relationships in rural life are governed largely by local custom. Such communities still adhere to the modes and mores typical of primary groups with their low mobility and disengagement from modernisation processes. How such communities work can be vividly illustrated by Janki, a village in the direct vicinity of Warsaw. As the village is located at the exit road to Katowice and Cracow, the land around it proved attractive to French and Swiss investors. The in-flow of foreign buyers clearly beaconed bright prospects for the area, and indeed, Sweden's IKEA soon built a huge outlet there. The Janki farm owners were regularly solicited by investors, who bid millions of dollars for their land only to be sent away with a disaffected "well, what do I need with that cash, anyway?" for an answer (Mizerski 1996: 6). The Polish village to a considerable extent still seems a historical theme park – peasants put trust in land, remaining leery of money. Land proffers security while big money entails correspondingly big problems.

As individualistic attitudes became strongly related to occupational positions in 1998, it may suggest that differences in self-declared individualism were more closely intertwined with social stratification. It was paralleled by an increase in the association between individualism and education level, which generally tends to be more strongly correlated with attitudes and orientations than one's occupational position is. The correlation between individualistic orientations and the level of education increased from 0.23 in 1984 to 0.31 in 1998, which means that in 1998 knowing people's education, one could more accurately predict their inclination toward self-reliance.

A general finding that individualism is more strongly located in the occupational structure needs to be scrutinised in more detail since occupation depends on one's place of residence, age, sex and social origin; thus, its association with self-reliance may be contaminated by these variables. In order to establish a relatively "net" effect of occupation one should control for these factors. Table 4 contains partial correlation coefficients which inform about the relationship between individualistic attitudes and the respondents' sex, age, social origin, place of residence, income and, of course, occupational position – the values of correlations are multiplied by 100 to be interpretable as percentages. The figures show the effect of each of these variables on individualism, after controlling for the impact of the remaining ones. Education is not included in the analysis because of its strong association with the occupational category – if both these characteristics had been taken into account, it would not have been possible to specify correctly their respective effects.

Table 4: Relationship between self-reliance and selected individual characteristics. Partial correlation coefficients (multiplied by 100)

Individual characteristics	Self-reliance (%) in:	
	1984	1998
Father's socio-occupational category	0.1	1.3
Respondent's socio-occupational category	1.5	1.6
Sex	1.4	0.2
Age	1.4	2.1
Family income per capita (logarithm)	2.6	0.5
Size of the place of residence	1.5	0.2
R^2	9.4	13.5

The R^2 (multiple correlation) given in the bottom row of Table 4 shows the total impact of individual characteristics on self-reliance.[3] We see that the

---

3   In the regression model presented in Table 4, the dependent variable is the respondents' position on the self-reliance scale. To facilitate interpretation, the original scores for this scale were converted so as to render a 0-100 scale. Concerning the independent variables, membership in an occupational category is defined by a set of seven dummy variables consisting of: (i) the intelligentsia and senior managerial staff, (ii) lower-ranked white collars, (iii) owners, (iv) skilled workers, (v) unskilled workers, (vi) farm owners and agricultural workers, and (vii) sales and services as a reference category. The father's occupational category, which identifies the effect of social origin, is identified in the same way. The size of the place of residence is an 8-point scale which reflects the number of inhabitants in thousands (ranging from villagers who were arbitrarily ascribed the value of 2 to inhabitants of towns with the population above 500 thousand, who were assigned the value of 500). Family income is expressed as the average of monthly incomes of all family members per capita. Sex is a dummy variable (male = 1). Age is defined by 5 dummy variables (included in Table 5), with the oldest respondents (65+) taken as a reference category. Metric regression

association strengthened over the years 1984-1998 (the multiple correlation coefficient grew from 9.4 to 13.5), which seems to confirm that in 1998 certainty and self-confidence were more closely associated with one's general position in the social structure, defined in terms of sex, age, social origin, occupation, and family income consequent upon it. Although the impact of the social structure increased by one third, which is a substantial value, it still does not determine the level of individualistic attitudes. Having subtracted 13.5 from 100%, we are still left with 86.5% to account for. In conclusion, the location in the social structure significantly differentiates individualistic attitudes, but its impact is relatively minor.

Another conclusion specifically concerns the role of occupational divisions which are the quintessence of the stratification system and, as such, should matter. It turns out that no major changes took place in this respect. In 1984, occupational divisions "explained" only 1.5%, and in 1998 only 1.6%, of the total variation of individualistic orientations. This suggests that self-reliance was not more strongly embedded in social stratification (identified with the occupational hierarchy) although at the same time it was more deeply rooted in the social structure in its broad meaning. Differentiation of self-reliance among occupational categories did not significantly increase; certainly, its rise by a mere 0.1% does not indicate a growing importance of occupations. Given how prominent a role occupational career plays in overall life career in market societies, occupation could be expected to be relatively the strongest determinant of individualist attitudes. It is not, however, as both in 1984 and in 1998 membership in a socio-occupational category was not among the major determinants of self-reliance. In the 1980s, individualistic attitudes correlated the strongest with family income, while sex, age and the size of the place of residence differentiated them no less strongly than occupational position did. In 1998, in turn, age took precedence in this relationship, which implies that the political and economic transition enhanced generational differences. Certain age cohorts became more important exponents of individualistic attitudes.

coefficients for that category (Table 5) were derived based upon a slightly modified model which included the oldest respondents but omitted the youngest ones. The basic difference between models presented in Table 4 and Table 5 lies in operationalistion of the respondent's socio-occupational category. The model in Table 5 is a set of dummy variables which identify both people actively involved in the labour market in 1984 and 1998, as well as occupationally inactive categories: housewives, pensioners, retirees and students. Workers in sales and services represent a reference category, which is not included in Table 5.

Let us turn to more detailed findings. The data presented in Table 5 show relative declines and increments of self-reliance, depending on socio-occupational strata, categories of social origin, age and other characteristics. The "increments" and "declines" are expressed as coefficients of regression (derived from the model in Table 4), where positive values show what raised and negative values what lowered self-reliance in 1984 and 1998, after controlling, of course, for the impact of other variables.[4] In other words, these statistics reveal the strongest and the weakest linkages of individualism in the social structure.

Comparing these relationships for 1984 and 1988, we can identify the areas where downward tendencies in individualistic orientations prevailed. It appears that, as for age, capitalism diminished vigour mostly in the 30–40 cohort, in which individualistic attitudes decreased from 0.55 to 0.42 points (after controlling for all other characteristics). That notwithstanding, the generation of 30-year-olds stood out as the most self-reliant category. Individualistic orientations were slightly weaker in the youngest age cohort and the weakest in the oldest one. It suggests that individualists are to be found first of all among young people, which is consistent with another study on individualism in Poland (Giza-Poleszczuk 2000).

---

4   For the socio-occupational category of respondents and their fathers and for the age category, the regression coefficients identify the distance between the mean self-reliance score for each category and the overall mean (which is a result of using effect-coded dummy variables, see Cohen and Cohen 1983). For example, the value of 0.42 in 1998 indicates the "net" distance between people aged 30–40 and the mean for the total sample of adult Poles on the 100-point self-reliance scale.

Table 5: Relationship between self-reliance and selected social characteristics. Metric regression coefficients

Individual characteristics	Self-reliance	
	1984	1998
Father's occupational category:		
Higher managerial staff and intelligentsia	0.47**	0.14
Lower non-manual categories	0.25	0.14
Owners	−0.42	0.09
Foremen and skilled workers	−0.21	0.10
Unskilled workers	0.36	−0.68**
Farm owners and agricultural workers	−0.21	−0.20
Sex (male)	0.73 **	0.19
Age:		
18–29 years	0.24	0.19
30–40 years	0.55**	0.42**
41–49 years	0.15	0.16
50–65 years	−0.59**	−0.35**
plus 65 years	−0.35	−0.42
Respondent's occupational category:		
Higher managerial staff and intelligentsia		0.56**
Lower non-manual categories	0.56**	0.45**
Owners	0.00	0.23
Foremen and skilled workers	0.40	−0.20
Unskilled workers	−0.56**	−0.44
Farm owners and agricultural workers	−0.89**	−0.36
Students	−0.08	0.95**
Home-makers	−0.08	−0.39
Pensioners	−0.10	−0.60
Retirees	0.11	−0.09
Size of the place of residence	0.47	0.95**
Family income per capita (logarithm)	0.48**	0.24**
Constant term	9.33	8.30
R^2	0.08	0.15

**p<0,01; *p<0,05.

In 1984-1998, the effect of family income on individualism declined from 0.48 to 0.24. In 1998, each 100 Polish zloty in family income resulted in an increase of 0.24 on the self-reliance scale; nevertheless, the relationship between these variables was also less pronounced than in 1984. As for sex, males were, unsurprisingly, more individualistically oriented than females, but admittedly, their advantage in this respect had also dwindled. The biggest changes took place in the categories which are permanently absent from the labour market. Pensioners dropped to the bottom level of individualism, and students advanced the most – in 1998 they topped the hierarchy, even overtaking the occupational elite, that is, the intelligentsia and senior managers. Students made an incredible upward leap from 0.08 points below to 0.95 points above the national average. In 1998, being a student entailed a pronounced advantage in terms of self-reliant attitudes as compared to the statistical Pole.

It can be hypothesised that the advantage of students crystallised directly after the systemic change. As early as in 1991, students were found to declare more confidence in their capacities than senior managers, the intelligentsia and other social categories (Domański and Dukaczewska 1997). According to the data from a study carried out on a national sample, this tendency was discernible also in 1995. Since the same pattern was observed in 1998, it can be concluded that in the early 1990s individualistic attitudes of students were powerfully boosted.

My interpretation is as follows: students with their sparse life experience are more likely to overestimate their chances for success. Their optimism is linked with high self-esteem and the acquisition of specialist qualifications, which fosters hopes for a spectacular career. Characteristically, upper managers and the intelligentsia scored lower than students, likely successors to their occupational status, which implies that the highest self-reliance of students stems from their buoyant visions, which are bound to mature and become more realistic in time. Furthermore, a strong inclination toward self-reliance is not necessarily a permanent trait of this category: self-declared individualism of students surfaced only in the 1990s, a period which sparked hopes for personal development and career opportunities.

To return briefly to changes in the other categories of the social structure – individualistic attitudes grew among lower non-manual workers, while they declined among business owners and the agricultural categories. At the same time, we witnessed an increase in the effect of social origin: in statistical terms, the relative "share" of the paternal socio-occupational stratum in explaining individualistic attitudes picked up from 0.1% to 1.3%, and in 1998 it was only slightly lower than that of the respondents' occupational category. Social origin shaped individualistic attitudes according to a typical pattern, consistent with the socio-economic position. Senior managers and specialists took the top places while farmers and workers trailed at the bottom of the stratification ladder.

Based on these findings, one can draw a few conclusions. The most important one concerns the directions of development. Namely, the early phase of capitalism in Poland did not activate orientations which typically fuel entrepreneurship in developed market economies. Essentially, self-confidence, as Table 3 implies, was thwarted also in the categories expected to lead the changes, that is, in the intelligentsia, senior managerial staff and business owners, in which, surprisingly perhaps, "faith in good (but external) luck" and reluctance to "start from scratch all over again" consolidated rather than subsided. Similar attitudes spread also among workers and farmers, which was not highly significant, in fact, because workers are mere routinised performers of occupational roles and the peasant mentality is moulded by fatalism and aversion to change.

In an analytical overview of these processes, we must conclude that their implications are different for the stratification system and for individuals themselves. For social stratification, self-declared individualism mattered the same in the 1980s and the 1990s, because no major changes took place in the magnitude and patterns of relationships between a proclivity for self-reliance and the socio-occupational position. In terms of individual behaviours, these attitudes mattered less as evidenced by a decrease in their declared strength. These tendencies are in accord with the analyses carried out by Marek Ziółkowski (2000: 224), who used the data from national surveys launched in 1988 and 1998. Briefly, the capitalist market mechanisms did not enforce inclinations toward self-reliance on the level of self-declared opinions.

Sources of Dejection

Given the inherent stability of social stratification, it is hardly surprising that no significant changes in the position of individualistic orientations in the social hierarchy have come to pass. What is indeed more surprising is that these attitudes declined in the 1990s. Predictably, they should have been stronger than in the 1980s but, patently, they were not.

Let us revisit historical roots. From the very beginning, America was colonised by people who had left behind social barriers erected by the European estate system. While in France and England the most resourceful individuals were satisfied with the hierarchical order, in America individualism was "positive" as it ensued from the conviction that rigid social hierarchies were irrational, inequitable and unacceptable. With their expansionist spirit and audacity, the settlers were ready to face up to all threats and had no fear of moral defeat, though they knew they could fail in life. The United States was infused with the idea of a self-made man, a career pattern intensely eulogised and promoted. American advertising savvies invented the lone hero figure, with Raymond Chandler's private detective Philip Marlowe and Gary Cooper's rendition of the sheriff in *High Noon* being but two examples in a copious gallery of such types. Difficult to live with perhaps, but certainly appealing and likeable, the protagonists take up a fight against all odds and emerge proudly victorious at the end. Such examples emphatically teach the middle-class hopeful how, though starting from an apparently no-win situation, an individual can nevertheless find the right track. Polish literature and film have never created a determined figure who rebounds from any blow like Humphrey Bogart does in *The Maltese Falcon*.

For American individualism to be successfully transplanted onto Polish soil, a few boundary conditions would have to be satisfied. The most important one is, undeniably, a rise in affluence. Individualistic attitudes are an attribute of the middle class, and nothing comes anywhere close to financial success in motivating diligent work, self-discipline and personal responsibility. Another condition would be the state's relinquishing of obligations which hamper individual entrepreneurial initiatives. Set afloat on unknown waters, people are compelled to navigate and cope with adversities by themselves.

The development of constitutionally sanctioned and legislatively asserted political individualism would be still another factor. The United States abides by the classic principle of an individual's freedom to think, speak and pursue happiness by voting in elections, formulated by Thomas Jefferson, a co-author of the American constitution and equal opportunities ideology. When applied to contemporary Poland, these famous words sound admittedly artificial, yet the development of political individualism could marginalise the role of blind chance and foster a greater engagement in matters which depend on the aggregate decisions of sovereign individuals. Last, but not least, practicalities are also important – individualism would stand a greater chance if a more accountant-like mode of life set in, if profit-and-loss calculation became part of the daily routine. This would not require an ethical revolution in which the individual's interest would outweigh the communal interest. It would be just enough to remove the barriers which thwart innovators' efforts to implement such solutions. "Would be just enough," ay, there's the rub, because obviously "to start" is where the greatest difficulty lies.

Getting used to a life of calculation would seem a lesser challenge than dissuading Poles from a specifically Polish species of Catholicism – a veritable contradiction of the self-reliance which is so powerfully endorsed by the Protestant denominations and so deeply ingrained in developed market societies. In attempts to identify impediments to individualistic leanings, we should consider the following contention: "I understand a Catholicism such as the one that has historically developed in Poland as the shifting of burdens beyond one's own powers to someone else – God. This is entirely the relation of children to their father. […] This way, the Pole gained a green world, green because it is immature […]." The same author believes that Poles would like "[…] to live in the lap of nature, in a limited world, leaving the black universe to God." The passage comes from the first volume of Gombrowicz's *Diary* (2012: 218), which he wrote as an émigré with the overt purpose of belittling national symbols in intentionally scornful diction and derisive reflections. Gombrowicz was a determined advocate of universalism and a relentless critic of what he considered bigoted behaviours and attitudes.

For an external observer and supporter of modernisation, Polish Catholicism comes across as a blend of mysticism and parochial mentality, which contrasts sharply with the open-minded attitudes to faith prevalent in the West. One reason why America still continues to be a promised land is its extreme (in a sense) determination to ensure freedom of worship. An average American neither thinks of a church as a temple nor sees a creed as ascribed to a person once and for all; religious practices are a matter of individual choice rather than of collective ecstasy. Although American Catholicism demands committed allegiance to the Church, the congregation tend to identify with the mundane problems their parish copes with, remaining remarkably flexible toward the papal authority, bishops, ritual gestures and the ecclesiastical hierarchy (Fee et al. 1981). Such autonomy is encouraged by pluralism of local denominations. Research suggests that American worshippers pay more heed to the private reading of the Bible than to the great authorities of the Church.

Ever since *The Protestant Ethic and the Spirit of Capitalism* was published, it has been a common consensus that Protestantism is more conducive to individualistic attitudes and the market economy. Whether or not Gombrowicz actually knew Max Weber's study, he anyway proclaimed that Catholicism gauged our immaturity, caused deprivation of personality and lured people into passivity. Based on the nation-wide study carried out in 1998 on a representative national sample, I attempted to test the hypothesis that greater religiosity is related to lower self-reliance. The study shows that, indeed, religiosity exerts a negative impact on dispositions toward self-reliance. Answering the standard question: "How often do you attend masses and services?" the respondents used a 7-point scale, ranging from "never" to "at least 1-2 times a week," where the latter represented the highest level of behavioural religiosity. The last of these categories exhibited the lowest tendency to rely on themselves in terms of our scale ranging from 4 to 16. The mean score of self-reliance among the most frequent church-goers stood at 9.2, growing to 9.3 for the respondents who went to church once a week at most, to 9.8 for those who attended the mass once a month at most, and reaching a record level of 10.2 for respondents indifferent to religious practices. However, it must be noted that religiosity is not a strong barrier to the development of individualistic attitudes, as the correlation coefficient between individualism and church-going amounts only to 0.13. The relationship is so weak that it does not suggest the specificity of the Polish context.

Emphatically, Western societies are not the same middle-class societies that they used to be in the past. Individualistic attitudes, constitutive of the spirit of capitalism, are now less austere and less compulsive. We could say that individualism has been put up for reassessment – the classical rigours of the Protestant ethics are being renegotiated, with the middle class acting as a chief "negotiator." The middle class may still practise intense self-reckoning, but they do it in ways which allow a reasonable compromise between the rationalisation of effort and the needs of consumption. Highly developed societies either do not want to or cannot afford to relinquish consumption. The original interpretation of the Protestant ethic was a rhetorical feat of zealous doctrinaires; now it is addressed in the spirit of resignation. And the main point to consider is how much of it can be abandoned without impairing the motivation for hard work necessary to prevent the growth rate from dropping, while the traditional middle-class mores and values are losing ground, beset by the temptations of comforts granted by affluence.

Criticism of individualistic orientations in Western societies targets three areas: medicine, hedonism and community. Let us consider to what degree these developments concern Poland. In this, we might be moving somewhat ahead of our time – we are only in the early stages of the transition to a market society and a quick transfer of individualistic attitudes is not to be expected.

Medical criticism, represented among others by Karen Horney and Erich Fromm, addresses the question of mental disorders. Drawing on psychoanalytical notions in the interpretation of social crises, Horney (1968) proposes that our epoch's distinctive feature is a neurotic drive for power, prestige and the possession of commodities, which – becoming values in and for themselves – cause pain and suffering to those who desire them. In his *Escape from Freedom*, Fromm focuses on the formation of totalitarian regimes in the period predating Horney's analyses. Individualism entails freedom, but freedom is bound up with new duties, anxieties and fears. As Fromm argues (1944), an escape from freedom is precipitated by confusion amidst a world devoid of norms and straightforward rules for living, which prompts a desire to cede all responsibility to some authority. Unquestioned authorities were supposed to guarantee restoring mental balance to people previously abandoned to vie for themselves.

In the case of Poland, there is no denying that the explosion of capitalism was a traumatic experience for many people, sweeping them off their feet and then leaving them to their own devices. However, it is highly unlikely to have yet produced individuals dazzled by freedom gone rampant. The 1990s tested adaptability to the exacting rules of the market rationality. While capitalism is certainly a more flexible system than the previous regime, in its early period it did not leave much freedom of choice to most people.

Clinician psychologists describe a compulsive drive to succeed as a classical case of severe neurosis. Research launched in the 1950s by a team of Yale University psychiatrists and sociologists found that stress and breakdown affected winners and losers alike, with incidence of depression, alcohol abuse and other related conditions reported in both groups (Hollingshead and Redlich 1958). In Poland, there is a growing demand for *outplacement*, therapeutic services which target all those who have failed to achieve a desired goal, especially people suffering from mental breakdowns induced by job loss. In outplacement, the emphasis is placed on improving self-assessment, recovering self-confidence, combating apathy and fostering reflection on further career possibilities. In the 1990s, these services grew exponentially. In Poland, their clients recruited mainly from among higher executives – ambitious, success-oriented individuals who in their relentless upward push did not envisage losing their plum jobs or being laid off. The sudden crisis of 1998 was enough to force the realisation that to pick oneself up after tumbling all the way down from an air-conditioned top-floor office is an art as important as getting there in the first place. In the lower classes, which experience fewer agonizing downfalls, sober reconciliation with fate is the order of the day. A manual worker spelled it out to me in a short conversation once (not that I needed research to know it): "My brother is a director in a big company, he's a big fish, and sneers at such losers as me... But, I'll tell you what, our neighbours downstairs are pretty bad-off. He is a joiner only, but he never gets mad, like my brother does, and isn't nervy; he earns little money, but he doesn't seem to mind that terribly."

The second criticism of individualistic orientations targets hedonism. The "hedonism" critique blames individualism for the pathologies alleged to plague life style. Hedonism is habitually used to refer to pleasure-seeking combined with excessive consumption, exhibited in refined surfeit and an unseemly lack of self-control. Individualism is accused of making people fall for the allures of the expansive mass culture and choose the plethora of wrong options it disseminates – peruse comic strips instead of serious books, watch soap operas and reality shows rather than quality TV programmes and indulge in extravaganza (like wearing gaudy patterned ties). The ruinous impact of individualism transpires in decadence, the erosion of entrepreneurship, the demise of genuine elites, a loss of guidelines in life and self-admiration called narcissism by Christopher Lasch (1982). The list of individualist demerits includes also immoral ostentation, the crisis in Western democracies, the dissolution of ethical rigours and, ultimately, a collapse of the Protestant ethos (Bell 1976; Bellah et al. 1986; Lasch 1982; Sennett 1998). Clearly, individualistic attitudes have been painted a gravedigger of the ideology which symbolised their rise.

Relating these observations to Poland, we should notice that, firstly, GDP per capita in our country is ten times lower than in the USA, which prevents, at least for now, the development of ostentatious, pathological life style forms. We are not likely to blindly indulge in delights and make a dog and pony show of sumptuous consumption. Secondly, swelling hedonism is a fruit of excessive individualism while in Poland individualistic attitudes have not surged.

The third type of criticism exposes the detrimental influence of individualism on civic engagement and a feeling of community. It especially indicts the nihilistic manifestations of individualism that can be seen in Western societies in the corruption of state officials and abuses of administrative power. The "communal" critique also involves two other aspects – a pragmatic and an emotional one. In pragmatic terms, individualistic strategies are alleged to generate greater social and financial costs as compared to solutions undertaken in the spirit of collective collaboration; for example, to hire a nanny is more expensive than to have a kindergarten organised by a neighbourhood community. Collective action is also more effective because goals are attained more easily by exerting group pressure, for example, on employers or the government. In less pragmatic and more emotional terms, individualism is found culpable in dissolving social bonds and, consequently, in depleting the resources of psychological support available for people who need assistance and friendship on an everyday basis.

The main problem lies in reconciling private interests and the public good, although the founders of "liberal individualism" articulated among others by John Stuart Mill did not see the two as contradictory. Mill contended that civic good is a sum of the pursuits of rationally thinking beings, which suggests that in tending to private interests one learns to recognise the interests of the state or of a neighbour community. In Poland, the main dilemma is, rather, how to "individualise" Poles. The notion that individualism, self-interest and selfishness contributed to the partitions and the loss of an independent Polish state in 1795-1918 has formatively impressed itself upon our awareness and still lingers, whereas American individualism took shape under the influence of doctrines espousing individual freedom. Poles were convinced that national sovereignty could be regained only through collective effort. The Solidarity trade union programme foregrounded ideas of self-government and democratic dialogue. How pertinent such thinking still is can be seen in the Polish bishops' address to the nation and the government issued in December, 2000: "The Church reminds and urges all those responsible for changes in Polish realities, both to the right and to the left of the political scene, to collaborate in the spirit of solidarity for the furtherance of common good. What we need is all citizens and all political parties agreeing on the fundamental principles of social life and enacting them together."

Even American individualism did not necessarily entail selfishness. The sheriff, after all, always fired his gun to protect the townsfolk. The lone hero fought for the community with selfless dedication. Robert Lane (2000) lists four dichotomies inherent in the capitalist system which exemplify a fundamental incongruity between communal attitudes and the drive for self-reliance: (i) close ties nullify the essence of impersonal contract; (ii) meritocracy precludes nepotism and family bonds; (iii) serving self-interest in making choices for life reduces commitment to the communal interest; (iv) economic account-settling, where profit-seeking prevails, leaves no room for friendship.

If "the fundamental principles" mentioned by the bishops are indeed at odds with individualistic orientations, we could explain in part the distressing stagnation in inclinations toward self-reliance. In the 1998 survey, the respondents were asked questions which pinpointed selected aspects of their sense of civic duty. We could assume that a lack of correlation between these attitudes and their declared self-reliance would prove that there is no contradiction – the respondents were asked to specify how much they condemned "going by train or municipal transport without paying the fare," "refusal of army service," "tax evasion" and "a city councillor skipping his duty hours." It turns out that there is no relationship between the negative assessment of such behaviours and inclinations towards self-reliance. Strictly speaking, there is a correlation, but it is a curvilinear one as both the most and the least reproving assessments of such behaviours were associated with a relatively lower declared self-reliance, while the biggest individualists avoided extremes in their outstandingly moderate judgments.

Individualistic attitudes matter as much to the middle class as ownership and decent income. In comparison with the 1980s, Poles declare less pronounced inclinations toward self-reliance. To interpret this finding accurately, we need to place it in the international context. Differences between Poland and developed market societies are brought to light by the results of national surveys carried out in 1986-1993 in 12 capitalist countries to investigate "inner-directedness" of managers. To establish in which country self-confidence is the strongest, the respondents were asked to make a choice in five pairs of opposite statements. The results showed that Americans were the biggest individualists, with 68% of the sample declaring the highest inner-directedness. They were followed by Germans (65%) and Canadians (64%) in second and third place, respectively; the middle positions were taken by the Dutch (55%), Italians and Belgians (49%), with managers from Singapore (42%) and Japan (41%) scoring the lowest (Hampden-Turner and Trompenaars 1996: 55). No equivalent research has been conducted to examine Polish managers. What we do know is that Poles would be relatively more often inclined to expect governmental help. According to the World Value Survey carried out in 1993, 37% of the Polish sample agreed that "the government should take more responsibility to ensure that everyone is provided for." The first four places in this respect were taken by Chile, Latvia, Japan and Nigeria (54–55%). Among 42 countries covered by the study, Poland scored 16th before, among others, West Germany and the UK, with the USA (14%) and Sweden (11%) located at the bottom, i.e. displaying the highest self-reliance (Inglehart et al. 1998).

As no comparative data are available, we cannot establish to what extent Polish society exhibits less confidence in its efforts in other respects. Certainly, individualistic orientations, generally a driving force behind the success of market societies, have not consolidated. The readiness to take the helm of life in one's own hands has slid below the level reported for 1984, which is quite a paradox in terms of the norms of middle-class society.

Chapter IV: Aspirations and Value Systems

A fever of newness has been everywhere confused with the spirit of progress.

Henry Ford

The West looks on the world through the eyes of the middle class; that is, in the optics of class divisions, because to say that it looks on the world through the eyes of eco-activists or New-Left dissenters would be equally pertinent if another perspective were assumed. The universalist tradition of Western societies champions rationalism, democracy, faith in progress and respect for individual rights. Trying to identify such qualities in Poland, we will analyse changes in values which are more general than both individualism and the drive to succeed examined in the previous chapter.

American society puts a high premium on equality. This is manifest, for example, in dispensing with stiff formal manners, a practice popularly regarded as distinctly American. Employees and managers address each other as "you," camaraderie is fostered at workplace, and titles are dropped. The egalitarian model prevails in family and at school. Middle-class spouses tend to emphasise their equal partnership in marriage, important decisions are made jointly in the spirit of mutual understanding, and relationships with children are permeated with kind familiarity, eschewing authoritarianism and patriarchal gestures. In February 2001, when America celebrated Ronald Reagan's 90th birthday, the considerable media coverage of the event featured many guests who shared their memories. One of the renowned speakers was George Schultz, a former Secretary of the Defence, whom the host kept addressing as "George," which, it should be admitted, did not go down well with some viewers. Generally, however, to pat the US President on the shoulder is not considered a faux pas or an offence. A noble postulate for "every man to be his own master" is treated as a test of constitutional rights. During the presidential campaign of 2000 (George Bush vs. Al Gore), a carefully directed spot showed Gore – canvassing for votes, dressed casually and, from a distance, resembling a postman – walk up the porch of a suburban house, knock on the door and patiently wait to be answered. All that was designed to convince the viewer that in America egalitarianism was the air breathed by all alike. American democracy has instilled a need for equal treatment and everyday kindness in the population.

In liberalism, freedom is understood first of all as freedom from constraints imposed upon individual liberties. Emphasis is placed primarily on exemption from coercion, that is, on "freedom from," referred to as "negative freedom" in Locke-inspired liberalism. It is a freedom from authority and power. The notion of "positive freedom," in turn, entails conferring rights upon people and ensuring social security. Public opinion polls provide convincing evidence that the members of Western societies give freedom precedence over equality and other universalist values. When asked to name the greatest advantages of the democratic governance system, they enumerate freedom of thought, freedom of expression and inalienable freedom of religion. Also in Poland, freedom turns out to outweigh equality. In 2000, 52% of those polled by the CBOS stated that if made to choose between equality and freedom, they would opt for the latter; while 37% preferred equality. Liberal preferences are possibly on the rise in Poland, but "freedom" still tends to connote a right to free education, pension, employment, decent earnings and state-provided health care. The habits inculcated under the former regime are still in place.

It is commonly believed that the ubiquity of middle-class values in Western societies makes studying them altogether redundant. Below, we will try to trace them in Poland, examining tolerance and approval for unequal pay. The liberal worldview and the principle of performance-based differentiation of rewards are associated with respect for individual rights and endorsement of the harsh rules of the market economy. This distinctive syndrome of attitudes is entrenched in middle-class societies. Middle-class members generally tend to be more fervent supporters of the market mechanisms than the lower classes, approach women's emancipation more liberally and are more tolerant in such thorny matters as homosexuality, marital infidelity and premarital sex. The main question to be answered here is whether an average Pole's take on these issues is coming to resemble the typical middle-class approach.

Tolerance

Sex-related inequalities are founded on assigning males to the public sphere and females to the domestic one. In the wake of the feminist revolution (which is often said to be still in progress), expressing a disapproval of working women counts as a proof of the traditional belief that the home is a woman's proper place. Women's commitment to family and the hearth, De Tocqueville wrote (1954 ed.), is commendable because the home is a refuge of peace and concord amidst the tribulation-fraught world of work and public involvements. De Tocqueville formulated such insights in *Democracy in America*, probably the first sociological monograph study of the middle-class society. As his followers picked up and developed that notion, the apology of family and traditional division of roles promoted by pulpit ideologies crystallised into a vision of a social hierarchy in which a wife-and-mother is always superior to a working woman. Women's occupational engagement outside the home is reviled as detrimental to morality, which ties in closely with the critique of individualism, preoccupation with achievement and the compulsive career-drive. The selfless love of a wife and mother for her husband and children is a direct opposite of cold calculation and heartless utilitarianism, according to the authors of *Habits of the Heart*, a sociological bestseller from the 1970s (Bellah et al. 1986: 89). Pleading to mend family relationships in the patriarchal spirit, they crown this strand of their reasoning with an adulation of "unselfish love" of women who give up on their own careers.

The two world wars turned women's presence on the labour market into a hot issue. Each of the wars saw males join the army and industry strive to replenish its drained supply of workers. A mass influx of women into industry, which ensued in the corresponding two waves, was soon to ignite struggles for gender equality. Feminist campaigners insisted that reducing women to household chores only relegated them to the margin and consolidated the superior social status of male bread-winners. Emancipatory ideology averred that women's work outside the home could increase their prestige, enhance their economic independence and give them access to strategic goods, thereby undercutting the male monopoly. It also afforded a chance to dismantle men's traditional authority of the head of the household and to help working wives become their husbands' equal partners.

The interest in women's emancipation through work has prompted research which suggests two conclusions. The first conclusion makes it very clear how far Poland trails behind Western societies in the basic matter of ascribing certain social roles to women. Relatively recent insights are provided by the 1994 *International Social Survey Programme* carried out in 24 countries, therein Poland. The respondents were presented with a series of statements which reliably identify the attitude to women's empowerment through employment. Two items are particularly useful in grasping the degree of approval for the traditional gender roles: "A job is all right, but what most women really want is a home and children" and "Being a housewife is as rewarding as working for pay." The items aimed to force the respondents into a somewhat artificial situation of having to choose between the home-maker role and independence in order to avoid superficial declarations which are easily confusable with people's entrenched attitudes when they answer questions about preferences. The respondents, both male and female, were asked to represent their opinions on a five-point scale: "I strongly agree," "I agree," "I neither agree nor disagree," "I disagree," "I strongly disagree."

The comparison of the respective proportions of women's employment advocates and family-focused orientation supporters showed that pro-occupational preferences were the strongest in Western societies. The opposite pole of the spectrum was occupied by the post-communist countries and the Far East (represented by the Philippines and Japan), where the preferences for the traditional gender-roles division surpassed the occupational activity model. The Philippines was an extreme case with the home-maker model endorsed by the absolute majority – 57.4% of women and 53.2% of men – while only 7.1% of women and 5.1% of men supported women's work for pay. In the six surveyed East- and Central-European countries, their mentality similar to the Asian type, tolerant attitudes were reported by the total 17.3% of women and 10.5% of men. This represented a striking difference from the analysed 14 Western democracies, where the mean percentages approximated 39% and 32%, respectively. In Poland, women's emancipation through work was upheld by 9.8% of men and 18.9% of women (Domański 1999: 85–86).

The other conclusion from the surveys is that in all the studied countries, women's employment is advocated first and foremost by the middle classes. People with university-level education and a relatively higher socio-economic position significantly more often support equal work opportunities for men and women. This holds true particularly for higher managerial staff, professionals and people with relatively high income. Middle-class spouses more often discuss their problems together and devote more time to each other than married people of the lower classes, who are more beset by subsistence problems. Husbands in higher and better-paid jobs appreciate psychological gratifications afforded by spousal equality and are, thus, more inclined to renounce the bread-winning monopoly, family headship and allures of control. That such attitudes and relationships were relatively the strongest in market societies is by no means a coincidence.

Clearly, in 1994, Poles' attitude to women's occupational emancipation diverged from the views espoused by middle-class societies nurturing the ideas of gender equalisation. In order to trace the later dynamics of support for the traditional model, I will draw on nation-wide surveys carried out on representative random samples. The respondents were asked to judge three propositions, stating in how far they agreed that: (i) a woman should "create conditions promoting the husband's occupational success rather than pursue a career herself"; (ii) "it is harmful for young children if their mother has a job"; and (iii) it is advisable that "men earn the livelihood and women look after children and the home."

The percentages of those agreeing with the statements are presented in Table 6. The dynamics of views on women's employment suggest that the desired changes in these attitudes are underway, as opposed to the stagnation in self-declared individualism. Ever since 1992, the percentage of people ascribing the homemaker role to women has been decreasing regularly, though it must be admitted that a considerable majority of Poles are still swayed by the argument that when mothers work, children's interests are infringed and families would fare better if women tended to the household and men earned the family livelihood. That latter view, emblematic of a traditional vision of family with woman as "the angel in the house," was reported by 75.6% of Poles in 1998, a considerable proportion, indeed, but evidently lower than 85.2% recorded in 1992.

Table 6: Support for the traditional model of woman's role. Distribution of responses in 1992–1998

"I agree" and "I definitely agree"	1992	1993	1995	1998
A wife should create conditions promoting the husband's occupational success rather than pursue a career herself.	46,0	40,6	39,2	32,9
It is harmful for a young child if its mother has a job.	75,1	71,7	70,4	68,7
Families fare better when the man earns the living and the woman looks after children and the home	85,2	82,8	79,7	75,6

Similarly, the notion that wives should sacrifice their occupational careers for the sake of their husbands' ("a wife should create conditions promoting her husband's occupational success rather than pursue a career herself") was increasingly rejected. In the 1990s, that belief abated more than the other surveyed convictions. While in 1992 46% of the total sample upheld that assertion, in 1998 the proportion stood at 32.9% only. Breaching the traditional, gender-based division of roles in marriage was most fiercely opposed by agricultural workers and peasants, while its abolition was most frequently advocated by the non-technical intelligentsia and even more by the middle-rank administrative staff and clerical workers (see Table 7). These two categories are, by the way, the most feminised ones, which largely explains why they supported the concept of women's emancipation. Notably, the idea of woman's commitment to the domestic sphere lost some of its appeal across all the basic categories of the social hierarchy and surfaced less markedly not only in the prospective middle classes, that is, the intelligentsia and business people, but also among workers and peasants.

It would suggest that the traditional image of a wife as a priestess of the hearth has lost its erstwhile lustre, its splendour has dwindled beyond repair, and in all probability there is no going back to it. The past decade witnessed a revision of values underpinning family life, which is characteristically illustrated in the declining belief that children suffer if mothers work. Care for the good of children, as the research findings suggest, does not eclipse appreciation for women's greater occupational activity. In 1992, 75.1% of the respondents agreed that a mother's job could be detrimental for a child, one chief argument advanced by the advocates of traditional values. In 1995, the group shrank to 70.4%, and in 1998 to 68.7%.

Table 7: Support for the traditional model of woman's role in socio-occupational categories (in %).

Socio-occupational categories	Proportion of responses "I agree" and "I definitely agree" that "a wife should create conditions promoting the husband's occupational success rather pursue a career herself"	
	1992	1998
Higher managerial staff and administrative officials	59.1	28.5
Non-technical intelligentsia	27.2	20.4
Technical intelligentsia	30.3	34.4
Technicians	42.0	35.3
Mid-ranked administrative staff	34.7	14.2
Clerical workers	25.0	17.6
Business owners	46.6	31.8
Sales and services	46.6	24.3
Foremen	37.5	45.9
Skilled workers	53.1	38.4
Unskilled workers in production	51.4	40.0
Unskilled workers in services	44.9	34.4
Agricultural workers	62.5	53.3
Farm owners	64.7	48.9

The parliamentary election in October 2001 was won by the Democratic Left Alliance (Sojusz Lewicy Demokratycznej), a post-communist leftist party. One certain thing about the party is that ever since it was founded, it has consistently campaigned for women's rights. When the DLA came into power, its pro-women slogans were soon translated into institutional arrangements: the government's office for equal status of men and women was set up, and its head, officially called the government plenipotentiary, immediately appealed to launch "positive discrimination" policies, starting with imposition of gender quotas, in particular for public election slates, boards of directors and other top positions. Positive discrimination might have more advantages than drawbacks, but social consciousness is definitely inimical to edicts. In Poland, tolerance increased, but its progress was not uniform or overriding. We will now look into tolerance in the realm of the norms for intimate relationships, where conservative moods prevailed and restrictiveness was on the rise.

Restrictiveness

The 1968 student rebellion, which swept across the West undercutting its system of values, drove home the message that the American middle class was morally corrupt. Renowned intellectuals and influential media figures echoed each other, endlessly dwelling on the ills of "permissiveness." Employed earlier in psychological discussions on childrearing, the term was suddenly on everybody's lips, reiterated in admonitions to the American middle class, in which a loosening of values had purportedly passed beyond the point where laxity threatened to unhinge the social system. Branded as the root of all evil and deplored, permissiveness was cited across contexts as diverse as the collapse of the authority of the Church, corruptibility of the judiciary and politicians, and an inadmissibly liberal take on sex. The critical tone was set by publicists affiliated with the New Right, such as, notably, Pat Buchanan, who was later to gain an unusual recognisability by running in all presidential elections from 1992 on. The conservative defenders of the Protestant ethos denounced secularisation, abortion, homosexuality and unbridled sex as perilous vices and berated feminisms as one more sin caused by women's selfishness. "George Washington was not a permissive individual [...] The U.S. did not begin as a permissive society," asserted one of *The Conservative Digest* authors, crowning his argument with a rhetorical entreaty to the readers: "Is it too late to go back to our beginnings?"

Generally speaking, however, democracies proclaim tolerance for different worldviews as one of their cornerstones. Research shows that the middle classes are more condoning toward abortion, homosexuality and other behaviours which traditional moral codes brand as offenses (Zipp 1992). Greater liberalism in people of higher status is, as a rule, explained by their greater sense of security, material stability and self-appraised prestige. The university-educated middle-class members tend to exhibit more openness to and acceptance of practices which defy conventional rules. In turn, the working classes, low-skilled people of wobbly status lacking mental reinforcement, blame deviants for their own failures. Equating indecency with sin, they are not easily swayed to tolerate non-standard behaviours breaching traditional norms.

How about Poland? To trace configurations of moral tolerance in recent years I will resort to judgments reported in national surveys in which questions on homosexuality, premarital sex and marital infidelity were asked. One may consider the proportions of responses that these phenomena are "always" or "nearly always improper" as representing the respondents' condemnation (Table 8). The comparison of the data for 1992-1998 leads to an unambiguous conclusion that, in the 1990s, the conservative mores consolidated and Polish society grew more severe towards manifestations of permissiveness observable in modern market democracies.

Table 8: Objection to homosexuality, marital infidelity and premarital sex between 1992 and 1998 (%)

Responses "it is always" or "nearly always improper" if	1992	1993	1995	1998
Two people of the same sex have sexual relationships	66.2	66.7	73.4	72.4
A married person has sexual relationships with a person other than his/her wife/husband.	74.8	79.3	82.1	85.8
A woman and a man have sexual relationships before they are married	19.4	18.8	19.5	28.2

The data imply that marital infidelity is the most disapproved-of behaviour. In 1992, answering "What is your opinion on a married person's sexual relationships with a person other than his/her wife/husband?" 74.8% of respondents stated that "it is always" or "nearly always improper." In 1998, the proportion of the opponents of marital infidelity increased to 85.8%. The percentage of the detractors of same-sex relationships grew as well, even in the non-technical intelligentsia – the group declaring the most tolerant attitudes – with a majority disapproving of it (Table 9). On the national level, negative appraisals of homosexuality picked up from 66.2% to 72.4%. An increase was similarly noted in the disapproval of premarital sex. Even though it represented the most tolerated divergence from the traditional norms, premarital sex was reproved by 19.4% of the respondents in 1992, by 19.5% in 1995, and by 28.2% in 1998.

Table 9: Objection to homosexuality in socio-occupational categories (%)

Socio-occupational categories	Percentage of responses "it is always" or "nearly always improper" if two adult people of the same sex have sexual relationships	
	1992	1998
Higher managerial staff and administrative officials	50.0	78.5
Non-technical intelligentsia	51.5	55.5
Technical intelligentsia	50.0	71.9
Technicians	60.8	74.8
Mid-ranked administrative staff	60.9	59.9
Clerical workers	70.9	68.8
Business owners	60.9	61.0
Sales and services	70.0	66.9
Foremen	65.2	79.2
Skilled workers	60.1	78.5
Unskilled workers in production	70.8	83.0
Unskilled workers in services	75.1	78.5
Agricultural workers	69.7	84.3
Farm owners	60.9	87.0

These tendencies may reflect various attitudes. An interesting insight is offered by the following passage in Robert Pucek's column in one of May 2001 issues of *Rzeczpospolita*: "I'm not going to conceal that I'm one of those who consider homosexuality a disease (like Aristotle), an act that displeases God (as the Bible says) and an intent the enactment of which, for the simple reason of anatomical arrangements, flouts common sense [...] I'm also distressed that the public have a jargon of political correctness (the way I see it, the notion of "sexual minority" as related to homosexuals makes as much sense as labelling illiterates "a literary minority" while "love differently" sounds like "hate" to me) imposed on them by the circles whose philosophy, films, talk-shows and reportages strive to convince us that a white heterosexual (God forbid, Christian) male is a drunkard, a wife-batterer and a child molester."

More restrictive moral outlooks were accompanied by a less liberal attitude to foreigners and lower tolerance for beliefs held by various minorities. Later surveys carried out by the CBOS show that the proportion of people stating that "foreigners who do not accept our government should not stay in Poland" grew from 47% to 57% between 2000 and 2001. At the same time, the percentage of the opponents of excessive liberalism grew as well. While in March 2000 the percentage of those agreeing that "the principle of a universal right to abide by one's own opinions is unduly observed nowadays" stood at 33%, by June 2001 it rose to 41%. Interestingly, the authoritarian inclinations were not paralleled by a growing support for the authoritarian government system. Nearly three fourths of the total adult population declared that "though democracy has its drawbacks, no better system has been invented yet." Those who shared that opinion accounted for 74% of the respondents in 1993 and for 73% in 2001. Simultaneously, the percentage of those claiming that "a bit of dictatorship has never done any harm, and it's high time someone strong taught the quarrelling parties and officials a lesson" dropped from 71% to 34% (CBOS 2001: 10, 12).

These tendencies may be construed as confirming Poles' traditionalism and conservatism, but they may equally well be interpreted as bespeaking an edifying faith in the moral code and support for democracy. To make fuller sense of the findings, we also need to consider which categories report particular attitudes. Upper white collars and business owners were relatively less rigorous on breaching moral norms than manual workers and peasants. If we assume that liberalism of the Polish intelligentsia matches the attitudes of the Western middle classes, this finding might be a hopeful harbinger for the future.

Backing for the Market Rules

Inequalities of incomes are in the best interest of the middle classes because they help them find the meaning of life in tangible tokens of success. The welfare state model can hardly be favoured by people who reject collectivism and prioritise individual strategies for life. Hence, middle-class members have their reservations about governmental regulation of wages, state interventionist policies and increasing welfare expenditure, even though in American public opinion polls, in which the respondents were to choose between cutting military spending and curbing social welfare funds, most of the surveyed Americans sided with the opponents of the Pentagon (Ehrenreich 1989: 189). Conservative attitudes of the American middle class come to light most emphatically when their finances are at stake.

In order to establish common perception of the "just" inequality of incomes, I rely on the results of a survey carried out by the CBOS in March 2000. The respondents were queried whether "incomes from work should be: (i) considerably differentiated; (ii) a little differentiated; or (iii) not differentiated at all." Only 15.1% of the respondents opted for a considerable differentiation of incomes, and 11.7% believed that incomes should not be differentiated at all, while a substantial majority (68%) endorsed a moderate income differentiation, preferring "a little differentiated" incomes. 71.8% of the sample wanted the government to set a limit on incomes while 22.5% rejected the idea.

Table 10: Lack of acceptance for income inequalities. Distribution of opinions in 1992–1999.

Responses "I definitely agree" and "I rather agree" that:	1992	1993	1995	1998	1999
Income differences in Poland are too big	80.8	82.9	80.7	89.0	91.7
The government is responsible for reducing the difference between low and high incomes	73.1	75.1	72.2	82.9	89.2

Polish society, which in the 1990s wished to achieve prosperity without incurring any costs, instinctively denounced income inequalities, their distrust a legacy of the former system. In 1992, 80.8% of those polled in the Polish General Social Survey firmly denounced the existing income inequalities as too big. The proportion persisted into the mid-1990s to rise to 91.7% by 1999 (Table 10).[5] The group supporting policies for reduction of income inequalities was not much smaller. Asked whether "the government is responsible for reducing the difference between high and low incomes," 73.1% of the adult population sample answered "yes" is in 1992. In 1995, the proportion stood at 72.2%, and rose to 89.2% in 1999. Clearly, the discontent with unequal incomes went hand in hand with the acceptance of redistribution of incomes by the government, and the two attitudes tended to reinforce each other.

To trace changes in these attitudes over a longer period of time, I will use the available data from the 1980s. In a study carried out on a national sample in 1984, the respondents were asked two very similar questions: one about the existing income inequalities and the other about the expediency of governmental measures to curb them (see Adamski et al. 1986). One may hypothesise that the disapproval of considerable income inequalities combined with the support for income redistribution by the government would be inopportune in view of the emerging middle class in Poland. The study shows that in 1984 people who assessed the income inequalities as too big and, at the same time, believed they should be reduced made up 48.8% of the sample; in the 1990s, this category accounted for 86.7%, which reveals a crystallisation of these attitudes in time. Notably, resolved upholders of the hard-line course of market-oriented transformations were a

---

5   The 1999 survey was carried out by the Institute of Philosophy and Sociology at the Polish Academy of Sciences on a random nationwide sample of Poles aged over 18 years (Domański 2000b).

small minority: the percentage of those who accepted the existing inequalities and opposed any governmental interventions decreased from 4.4% in 1984 to 2.7% in 1998. The distribution of these attitudes is presented in Table 11.

Table 11: Opposition to income inequalities in Poland in 1984–1998

"The government is responsible for reducing the difference between high and low incomes"	Income differences in Poland are too big	
	I agree	I disagree
1984		
I agree	48,8	10,0
I disagree	33,8	4,4
1998		
I agree	86,7	4,3
I disagree	6,3	2,7

It is common knowledge that Western societies are facing an identity crisis, rampant consumerism of the middle classes is decried as a hazard to the entrepreneurial spirit, and governmental welfare policies are acclaimed by the public. However, Western societies still abide by the norm of pragmatic backing for the market relations and endorse the hierarchy of incomes in a far greater degree than Poles do (Alwin et al. 1993). A substantial majority of average American citizens do not believe in the efficacy of welfare policies implemented by the government agencies and rather poorly assess their economic effectiveness, just like, in fact, most practices which stray from self-achieved socio-occupational success. In social opinion polls, 36% of adult Americans believed that the federal funding of welfare schemes would contribute only a little to making America more affluent, 42% stated that it would not help "at all," and two thirds were of the opinion that implementation of such programmes was a "serious problem" for the economy. Merely 6% believed that it would not be "a problem at all" (Wuthnow 1996: 45).

Similar views prevail in Germany. To illustrate this, let us turn to the comparable data from Germany (a national survey from November 2000) and Poland (a CBOS survey from March 2000). The respondents in both samples were asked whether "the government should be responsible for reducing income inequalities." In Poland, 60% of the sample answered that "it definitely should" while in Germany the corresponding proportion stood at 45%. The far higher endorsement of inequalities in Germany was decided by the inhabitants of the Western lands, in which the advocates of redistribution were in the minority (40%), whereas interventionist policies were advocated by the former-GDR population, with 65% opting for active governmental involvement in the issue (Wenzel and Zagórski 2001).

A surge of pro-egalitarian preferences is certainly inauspicious for a country, like ours, which has freshly commenced the building of the market structures. Poles were all of a sudden plunged into a confrontation with capitalism's hostile facets. The traumatic nature of the experience helps understand why Poles do not accept inequalities and other ordeals caused by the on-going economic transformation. The data presented in Table 12 suggest that senior managers, the intelligentsia and business people are regularly the least eager to adopt pro-egalitarian positions. These findings match the tendencies observable in Western countries, which is a bit comforting insofar as any signs of compatibility with patterns entrenched in more stable social systems assuage our concerns.

Table 12: Disapproval of income inequalities in socio-occupational categories (%)

Socio-occupational categories	Percentage of responses "I definitely agree" and "I rather agree" that "the government is responsible for reducing the difference between high and low incomes"	
	1992	1998
Higher managerial staff and administrative officials	34.8	50.0
Non-technical intelligentsia	48.5	61.1
Technical intelligentsia	61.8	81.5
Technicians	71.0	82.4
Mid-ranked administrative staff	66.7	75.9
Clerical workers	66.7	88.3
Business owners	45.2	63.4
Sales and services	81.4	70.0
Foremen	80.4	88.5
Skilled workers	81.0	89.1
Unskilled workers in production	78.3	86.0
Unskilled workers in services	76.3	91.4
Agricultural workers	90.9	73.3
Farm owners	89.6	85.8

Aspirations and Social Status: Poland's Alignment with the Universal Trend

First systematic evidence on how value systems contribute to the reproduction of the class barriers was provided by Herbert Hyman (1954). In his article "The Value Systems of Different Classes," Hyman showed that, as compared with the middle classes, the working class members were less able to understand mechanisms of career and success, had lower educational aspirations, less ambitious plans for occupational careers and modest income expectations, and were less confident about the possibilities of social advancement. Hyman's analyses led to a spectacular conclusion that inequalities are reproduced with the consent of the socially disadvantaged people.

Research into psychological obstacles to social advancement and class mobility initiated by Hyman has effectively corroborated the thesis that aspirations follow a hierarchical pattern and overlap with socio-economic positions. We will see that also in Poland the educational and occupational aspirations of various social strata form a typical stratificational ladder, in which senior managers and the intelligentsia occupy the top and the working classes together with agricultural categories the bottom rungs.

Certainly, this hierarchical distribution of aspirations is not a specific product of the capitalist market. As early as in the 1970s, Hyman's hypothesis was confirmed also for Poland (Nowakowska 1977), although in those days the aspirations were in line with the modes of the communist society, in which employment was securely fixed. Studies of aspirations under the previous regime supplied, at most, some food for academic reflection on value systems dissociated, however, from the actual realities of life. In the 1990s, when good jobs were harder to come by, educational and occupational aspirations came to be more realistically related to newly emerging income and promotion opportunities. With professional expertise tested and rewarded by the market, a good occupation became a more likely source of satisfaction. Strikingly, the members of the lower classes do not seek to outdo upper status holders even in life plans although declarations about the future do not entail any actual obligations. The hierarchical pattern of aspirations is probably informed by the intuitive belief that everybody should know their place, succinctly encapsulated in an admonition not to step out of line.

Before we ascertain that this phenomenon is a universal one, let us consider its possible causes. In her attempts to understand why workers typically have low aspirations, Lillian Rubin (1992) attributes them to crucially formative workplace experiences and highlights the importance of "conformity" – a distinct trait of the mentality of manual workers – which fosters rigid thinking and strict adherence to the rules imposed top-down. The literature on these questions usually links conformist leanings to the occupational rigours and authoritarian methods of supervision at work. Kohn and Schooler (1986) contend that the habitual observance of norms in the workplace is extended onto other areas of life, which is reflected in childrearing practices and unshakable views. As early as in the 1950s, researchers who analysed the functioning of modern organisations noticed that careers in American industry characteristically followed two different paths: the "open" careers of white collars potentially led to the highest corporate positions while the "closed" career path was followed by workers, who could hope to wind up as foremen at best (Chinoy 1955; Seeley et al. 1956).

Workers' conformity, which can be coupled with a considerable sense of personal dignity, differs from thoroughly servile attitudes espoused by, as British sociologists put it, the deferential worker, which I addressed in the discussion of obstacles to individualism in the previous chapter. This once-prominent concept, developed particularly by Newby (1977), describes a very specific mentality in which unquestioned respect for people of high social status coalesces with a willing acceptance of one's own inferiority. In English society, deference was identified first of all among farm workers, but it is instrumental to the stability of any social system as a safety valve which "shuts off" potential excessive ambitions of lower-status people. This way of thinking is illustrated in an utterance by a respondent in Bernice Martin's study on workers' lives (1995): "When my mother finished school she wanted to work in a shop, but her parents said that our place is in the factory." In that case, a job in sales would entail social advancement, but people with fatalistic worldviews are shocked at the very idea of departing from their well-trodden career paths.

Wishes alone are not enough to make for life plans. These require also a realistic assessment of prospects based on the calculation of losses and profits. Cited above, Hyman's analyses (1954) show that workers, aware of financial constraints, do not formulate far-ranging educational plans for their sons and daughters. As prolonged education adds burdens to the family budget, male offspring go to work early to be financially independent of parents, and daughters are brought up to believe that early matrimony is their duty and best option. Irrespective of the pecuniary factors, the working-class culture is typically distrustful of such institutions as school. Workers are sceptical about education and convinced that children often waste time learning things of no relevance to their lives. The middle classes do not share such suspicions. Particularly, they do not view school as undermining their control over children, but rather as a suitable site for an early display of initiative and activity. For the middle classes, school is a preliminary test which initiates one into career-making efforts (McLeod 1987, Vanneman and Cannon 1987, Lamont 1992).

The chief conclusion these studies offer is that lower social status thwarts aspirations while the high social position promotes them, which can serve as a starting point for analysing this phenomenon as related to the formation of the middle class in Poland. I will focus on mechanisms which mould educational and occupational aspirations as indicated by the respondents' attitudes to their children's future. In a standard interview (within a survey carried out on a nationwide representative sample of adult Poles in 1998), the respondents were asked to "Imagine that your child has just finished elementary school and you are to choose the next school for him/her. If the choice was entirely up to you, what school would you send your son to: (i) none; he should go to work and learn the ropes of a trade; (ii) courses training in a particular occupation; (iii) basic vocational school; (iv) vocational secondary school or technical secondary school; (v) high school (i.e. general secondary school – *lyceum*)." Subsequently, the respondents were asked "What school would you send your daughter to?" with the same range of options to choose from.

The next two questions concerned occupational aspirations: "What would you like your son to do in the future, what occupation should he have? (If you have no son at this age, imagine that you do have one.)" An analogous question referred to aspirations for daughters.

Let us start from educational aspirations – school is, after all, the first link in a chain of events which formatively affect human lives and a decisive factor in placing people in the social hierarchy. The distribution of responses presented in the first two columns of Table 13 shows what proportions of the basic socio-occupational categories chose high school as a career-starting point for their sons and daughters. So far, all studies have proven that decisions made at this level of education determine the further career course. The choice of high school is tantamount to entering an upwardly mobile path: it facilitates enrolment at university and offers the best prospect for high occupational positions (Cf. Sawiński and Stasińska 1986, Shavit and Blossfeld 1993, Domański 2000a). Thus, aspirations related to this seminal decision reveal the hierarchy of values and, at the same time, put candidates to a test – a prelude to career.

As expected, high school tends to be chosen by senior managers, the intelligentsia, lower-ranked white collars and owners – the top categories of the stratification system. The proportion decreases, correspondingly, among manual workers and the agricultural categories, although skilled workers, on the average, go before the clerical staff in aspirations for daughters. In choices for sons, foremen stand out in scoring higher than technicians, clerical workers, business owners and obviously rank-and-file sales and services.

Apart from the visible impact of social stratification, striking in the distribution are sex-related divisions. High school was twice as often chosen for daughters as for sons: 62% of the sample declared choosing it for daughters, while only 31% for sons, which illustrates widespread differences in preferred career patterns for sons and daughters. That high school was chosen for daughters more often than for sons across all the socio-occupational categories proves that such preferences are fairly ubiquitous and uniform. And, indeed, in Poland far more females than males graduate from high schools, which implies that aspirations do affect actual choices. In 1998, 68.4% of people with high-school education were females, and 31.6% were males, as additional analyses of these data reveal.

Table 13: Proportions of the respondents choosing high school and extracurricular activities for their children

Socio-occupational categories	High school for:		Extracurricular, paid activities:	
	Son	Daughter	Sports	IT and computers
Higher managerial staff and administrative officials	57	86	69	69
Non-technical intelligentsia	78	89	84	78
Technical intelligentsia	47	88	68	74
Technicians	36	82	54	79
Mid-ranked administrative staff	48	71	56	80
Clerical workers	31	55	63	77
Business owners	38	78	62	88
Sales and services	23	56	59	74
Foremen	46	54	52	65
Skilled workers	23	62	55	73
Unskilled workers in production	24	51	45	71
Unskilled workers in services	25	43	51	63
Agricultural workers	20	40	38	67
Farm owners	23	51	43	72
Mean	31	62	62	88
Correlation ratio	0.29	0.26	0.18	0.13

The two right-hand columns of Table 13 show the percentage of the respondents who answered "yes" when asked "Would you arrange for extracurricular paid activities even if your child was a good student?" As in the high-school choice, upper managers, the intelligentsia, white-collars and business owners more often declared the readiness to incur additional costs for their children's education. Indeed, these categories tend to be more committed to equipping children with capitals which improve achievement opportunities, as compared with workers

and peasants. The respondents were presented with a list of additional courses for children, out of which the foreign language courses proved an absolute,
uniform favourite: they were chosen by 95% of the sample, with the percentage
never dropping below 92% in any of the analysed socio-occupational strata. The
most pronounced stratification is created by "IT and computers" and "sports."
The prospective Polish middle class seem to appreciate the advantages their children can derive from sports more than manual workers and peasants do, which
is probably a result of intercultural life style diffusion. Formed and implemented
by the middle class, the modern British schooling system has always credited
sports with a beneficial influence on self-discipline and health. The 19th-century
public school tradition enshrined rules of sporting rivalry and made the fair play
principle a cornerstone of its model of education.

High educational aspirations are a strategically important asset particularly
as employed by the intelligentsia, who owe their success primarily, though not
exclusively, to them. Let us turn to occupational aspirations and see whether
they are also related to the socio-occupational position. Table 14 includes the
mean values of occupational prestige scores for jobs to which the members of the
socio-occupational categories aspired for their sons and daughters. Why prestige? The scales of occupational prestige are a standard tool in measuring the
level of occupational aspirations in most studies. In cross-national research, several scales are used which comprise a few hundred detailed occupational categories assumed to reflect the common perception of social stratification. I used the
most popular of these scales – the Standard International Occupational Prestige
Scale constructed by Donald Treiman (1977).[6]

---

6 Originally, the scale ranges from 0 to 100 points assigned to a few hundred occupational categories based on the averaged scores of occupational prestige established
   in 60 societies. In all of the countries, an universal pattern emerges in which unskilled occupations have the least prestige and the opposite pole is occupied generally by occupations involving highly complex tasks, higher education and authority.
   The international invariance of occupational prestige permits to use it as a world-
   wide standard measure. Occupations chosen by the respondents for their sons and
   daughters were assigned scores from the SIOPS, which for the Polish sample ranges
   from 12 to 84.5.

Table 14: Mean values of occupational prestige of jobs chosen for sons and daughters

Socio-occupational categories	Means of prestige of occupations chosen for:	
	Son	Daughter
Higher managerial staff and administrative officials	71	69
Non-technical intelligentsia	72	67
Technical intelligentsia	69	71
Technicians	62	66
Mid-ranked administrative staff	69	67
Clerical workers	65	64
Business owners	61	66
Sales and service	61	65
Foremen	64	67
Skilled workers	61	64
Unskilled workers in production	57	60
Unskilled workers in services	56	60
Agricultural workers	49	55
Farm owners	57	60
Mean	62	64
Correlation ratio	0.31	0.23

Occupational aspirations are distributed across the social hierarchy upon a familiar pattern. The highest aspirations are reported by the intelligentsia: the non-technical intelligentsia choose for their sons occupations which, on the average, correspond to 71.9 points on the prestige scale; they are followed by senior managers. Occupational aspirations for daughters are similarly distributed, but the categories reporting the highest aspirations were closer to each other, and foremen (workers who supervise other workers) declared surprisingly high aspirations for their daughters, falling only slightly behind the technical intelligentsia. Agricultural workers trailed in the lowest position, reporting the least ambitious life plans for their children. The aspiration deficit is one of the psychological barriers which impede their development from the very beginning.

Similarly to different educational aspirations, sons and daughters have somewhat different occupational careers envisaged for them. The mean of occupational prestige in jobs chosen for daughters stood at 63.9 points, slightly above the mean value for sons (61.5). The effect of the child's sex on the parents' occupational aspirations for it is, thus, significantly lower than on the choice of high school, the latter being clearly the most "feminised" one. However, if aspirations were indeed a determining factor, men would occupy lower positions than women, which is an interesting insight for reversing the actual gender inequalities. Analogical findings were reported in the well-known study carried out in Wisconsin, USA (Sewell et al. 1970), which suggests that daughters are more appreciated in terms of declared values.

In Poland, this relationship does not spread uniformly across the social hierarchy – in particular, the non-technical intelligentsia and upper managers declared higher aspirations for sons. The privileged position assigned to sons by the respondents from the upper tiers of the occupational hierarchy sheds some light on the reproduction of sex-related inequalities. Higher aspirations for daughters reported by manual workers and peasants are likely to be less significant in confrontation with higher aspirations for sons reported by medical doctors or directors. Higher aspirations of the intelligentsia and senior executives have more thrust and are accompanied – as implied by the already cited studies by Rubin (1992) and Lamont (1992) – by more realism and determination, which increase the probability of future success.

Proponents of the cultural capital theory inspired by Bourdieu's empirical studies (1985) emphasise that accumulation of valuable capitals by the upper classes results from the intergenerational transfer of "culture," values and other resources related to life goals. In order to verify this statement, I regressed occupational prestige, which indicates occupational aspirations for daughters and sons, on the paternal occupational categories, the respondents' occupational roles and a few other variables. The results presented in the first two columns of Table 15 show to what extent social origin affected individual aspirations, irrespective of sex and age. The figures are coefficients of regression, which represent relative differences among aspirations of the respondents, depending on the categories of their fathers.[7] These values were also established after controlling

---

7   In the regression models presented in Table 15, the dependent variable is prestige of the occupation chosen for a son or a daughter. The occupations selected by the respondents were assigned scores from the International Occupational Prestige Scale (Treiman 1977). As for the independent variables, the respondents' occupational category was defined by 7 dummy variables covering: (i) the intelligentsia and higher managers; (ii) all other lower-ranked white collars; (iii) business owners; (iv) skilled workers; (v) unskilled workers; (vi) farmers and agricultural workers' and (vii) rank-and-file sales and services, who are a reference category omitted in the Table. The fathers' occupational category (when the respondent was aged 14), which identifies

for the place of residence, which is not presented in Table 15 as it was not signifi-cantly related to aspirations.

Indeed, the findings comply with Bourdieu's theory. Also for social origin, aspirations form a clear hierarchy, with individuals from the senior manager and intelligentsia categories on top, followed by children of lower-ranked white collars and business owners. Social origin translated into life plans nearly identically for sons and daughters, the only difference being that people stemming from the agricultural categories reported the lowest aspirations for sons, while children of unskilled workers relatively more often reported the lowest aspirations for daughters.

Table 15. *Relationship between occupational prestige of jobs chosen for sons and daughters and social origin, sex, age, occupational category, place of residence and school choice. Metric regression coefficients.*

Relationship with:	I		II		III	
	Son	Daughter	Son	Daughter	Son	Daughter
Father's occupational category:						
Intelligentsia	5.2 **	3.9 * *	0.4	1.5	−1.9	1.1
White collars	3.8 * *	3.1 * *	1.1	2.2	0.6	1.3
Business owners	1.0	0.5	3.2	1.4	3.5	0.5
Skilled workers	−1.4	−0.2	−1.2	−0.05	−0.8	0.2
Unskilled workers	−3.3 * *	−2.3	−0.9	−1.0	−0.5	−0.05
Farmers	−4.2 * *	−1.8	−1.5	−0.4	−0.7	0.2
Sex (1= female)	3.2 * *	−0.3	4.5 * *	−0.02	3.9 * *	0.02
Age groups:						
18–30 years	3.0 * *	1.0	3.8 * *	0.9	2.6 * *	−0.2
31–40 years	−0.3	0.3	0.4	0.3	1.1	0.01
41–50 years	−1.9 *	−1.3	−1.9 *	−1.1	1.4	−1.2

the impact of social origin, was identically defined. The size of the place of residence is an 8-point scale based on the number of inhabitants in thousands (starting from villagers who were arbitrarily ascribed the value of 2, to inhabitants of cities above 500 thousand, who were assigned the value of 500). Family income per capita is the aver-age of monthly incomes of all family members. Sex is a dummy variable (female = 1), as is "high school choice" added in the last model. Finally, age was defined in terms of 5 dummy variables (included in Table 15), where the oldest respondents (65+) serve as a reference category.

Relationship with:	I		II		III	
	Son	Daughter	Son	Daughter	Son	Daughter
51–65 years	0.4	0.8	–0.7	0.5	0.6	1.0
Respondent's occupational category:						
Intelligentsia	—	—	7.0 * *	2.0	3.7	1.1
White collars	—	—	3.1 * *	2.4	1.8	1.4
Business owners	—	—	–2.7	1.3	–2.5	0.6
Skilled workers	—	—	1.4	–0.08	–2.0	0.3
Unskilled workers	—	—	–5.1 * *	–3.8 * *	–3.3 *	–1.6
Farmers	—	—	–2.6 *	–2.6 *	–1.9	–4.2 * *
Family income per capita			0.004 * *	0.001	0.006 * *	0.000
High school choice			—	—	7.1 * *	5.6 * *
R^2	0.06	0.02	0.12	0.06	0.16	0.09

$**p < 0.01; *p < 0.05;$

Let us note that social origin affects aspirations for sons more strongly than aspirations for daughters. The comparison of regression coefficients across the father-categories for sons and daughters leaves no doubt that the declared expectations for daughters are less differentiated and, presumably, less strongly affect women's occupational careers, if we were to formulate general conclusions based on the data. This generalisation seems to be corroborated by American research reporting that educational and occupational aspirations for females are less determined by factors related to the social hierarchy (Sewell et al. 1979). As compared with aspirations for males, aspirations for females less depend on parental social status, occupational position and income. As is well known, men exert a critical influence on the shape of the social ladder and labour market mechanisms. The data presented here suggest that value systems contribute to these relationships.

Social origin underpins the intergenerational transfer of values in a specific way. It does not affect aspirations directly, but does so via the occupational position of offspring and other factors related to their career. This is evidenced in the statistically insignificant effect of paternal categories on the respondents' aspirations if their occupational position is taken into account (see models I and II). Briefly, having parents from the intelligentsia facilitates attainment of relatively higher positions, which in turn fosters correspondingly higher aspirations. At the same time, lower social origin is associated with inferior positions, thereby reducing, albeit indirectly, aspirations through undercutting hopes for and prospects of promotion.

Hyman's classical thesis – that aspirations are relative to status – is fully substantiated by the hierarchical distances between the intelligentsia, lower white collars, business owners, the working class and peasants. The regression coefficient values in the two right-hand columns of Table 15 show that the jobs chosen by the intelligentsia for their sons ranked 3.7 points higher than the mean on the prestige scale.[8] The 3.7-point distance is a fairly "net" effect of membership in the intelligentsia, which is conducive to strong motivations for success, high self-assessment and determination to retain the position that prompts one to achieve and excel. In terms of aspirations, the intelligentsia significantly prevails over the next category, i.e. lower white collars. The farthest behind are unskilled workers, whose jobs of choice for their sons stand 3.3 points below the mean on the prestige scale, after controlling for other characteristics. These relationships were less pronounced for daughters, with some other factors probably playing a role here.

These relationships could be more insightfully analysed if we established to what degree occupational aspirations resulted from other attitudes. Clearly, occupational aspirations are closely linked to educational aspirations as indicated by the declared choice of high school for a son or a daughter. On the prestige scale, the jobs chosen for sons by the respondents who appreciated high school education scored 7.1 points higher than the jobs picked by the respondents who did not opt for high school; in the case of daughters, the difference was 5.6 points. Such outcomes result from a number of causes. In all likelihood, one of them is the fact that people who from very early on learn how to pursue goals effectively are more realistic and more determined.

An additional commentary is in order about the role of sex, income and age. Income influences aspirations in ways similar to the occupational position, that is, higher income produces more expectations and incites greater ambitions. The effect of age is significant only in the case of sons and shows, basically, in the highest aspirations declared by the youngest respondents (below 30 years of age). Interestingly, aspirations turned out to be related to sex. Although females did

---

8   The values for respondent occupational categories, father categories and age categories can be interpreted as indicating the difference between the prestige of the chosen occupation and the mean for the overall sample. The interpretation is made possible by using effect-coding in which the coefficient values for categorical variables are relativised to the mean (unweighted) value.

not differ significantly from males in outlooks on their daughters' future lives, they chose emphatically more prestigious jobs (by 3.9 points) for their sons, which suggests that sons could rely on mothers rather than on fathers for support in occupational career.

Conclusions

The middle classes are distinguished by their value system, which enhances their well-being and fends off parochial views. In this chapter, we have focused on educational and occupational aspirations because middle-class members are constantly pressured to achieve and succeed.

The results of analyses presented above imply that in Poland, like in Western societies, people who take higher social positions have greater ambitions. In the 1990s, this rule was fully valid in Poland and could be seen in educational and occupational aspirations for sons and daughters. Membership in the intelligentsia, higher paternal social status and better income fostered relatively higher aspirations for children's education and jobs. A healthy instinct, values inculcated in socialisation and job satisfaction fuel the intelligentsia's resolve to maintain their position. This observation, however, does not justify drawing any far-ranging conclusions as to whether the intelligentsia have indeed absorbed middle-class values and attributes, especially since aspirations to high status have always been a defining feature of the intelligentsia even in the inauspicious realities of the planned economy. Such attitudes persist, yet occupational career designing is no longer as non-committal in thinking about the future as it was under the previous regime, when graduates had secure jobs guaranteed by the system, irrespective of their actual merits. Mechanisms of the capitalist labour market enforce far-reaching thinking and propel more ambitious individuals to develop long-term strategies exemplified in aspirations for children.

The first decade of building democracy saw a substantial growth of support for women's employment outside the home. In that sense, Poland seemed to be on the verge of embracing the emblematic liberal values and dismantling the patriarchal habits. However, at the same time, we witnessed a decline in liberalisation and an upsurge of support for traditional norms, which was reflected in the growing proportion of detractors of homosexuality, marital infidelity and premarital sex. This tendency was accompanied by a gradual withdrawal of approval for income inequality and an increasing endorsement of governmental social welfare policies. Like all societies working their way up, Poles wanted more state interventionism, which directly contravened the market rules and market-oriented attitudes.

Chapter V: The Old Intelligentsia vs. the New Middle Class

> Intellectuals suffer from their inability to alter the course of events. But they underestimate their influence. In a long term sense, politicians are the disciples of scholars and writers.
>
> Raymond Aron,
> *The Opium of the Intellectuals*

The class formation processes are structurally underpinned by occupational roles, relations of ownership and the labour market. Over the last hundred years, the development of the middle classes was fuelled by non-manual categories, in particular by highly qualified specialists, in the Anglo-American world referred to as *the professions* and – after C.W. Mills's *White Collar* was published in 1951 – as *the new middle class*, which gives it a more sociological ring.

Within the Polish social structure, their closest equivalent – and, probably, the hub of the new middle class – is the intelligentsia. The category owes its highest status and distinctive position to university education and its outcome – systematic, comprehensive knowledge. This is what makes, for example, surgeons surpass butchers, though, admittedly, a good butcher may be a meat-carving authority. This also lifts engine designers above car mechanics. Scrutinising various transformations within the intelligentsia, I will seek to answer some questions concerning the formation of a middle-class society in Poland which were left unexamined in the previous chapters. In doing that, I will focus on how the capitalist logic and the traditional ethos of the intelligentsia clashed in the 1990s and generated some new developments.

Old Problems vis-à-vis the Political Shift

The history of the intelligentsia is a history of their self-reflection, which typically flourished in times of crises. In 1927, Julien Benda published his *La trahison des clercs* – a critique of political engagement of the intellectuals and writers during the blooming days of democracy after World War One. In the period, people with reformatory leanings found political activism a tempting and enticing pursuit. In Benda's appraisal, the choice of propagandist and ideological involvements by a number of prominent personalities was an act of treason – a betrayal of the intellectuals' traditional ideals – which, consequently, precipitated a collapse of the authority of the creative professions. The harrowing dilemma of whether to opt for engagement or to linger in aloof neutrality was soon destined to leave the regions of literary ruminations and resolve itself in the confrontation of democracy and totalitarianism. The advocates of intellectual impartiality were left with one decision only – who to side with in this conjuncture?

Benda's argumentation acquired new pertinence in the late 1940s and 1950s, when a considerable portion of the intellectuals found an attractive alternative in communism, enacting in this way their predilection for contesting the social system, be it capitalism or the estate system. Many of them were later put in a predicament of reconciling universal values and responsibility for the crimes perpetrated by communism. The history of the intellectuals' alliance with the leftist movements was discussed in depth by Raymond Aron in *The Opium of the Intellectuals* (1957).

In the 20th century, the Polish intelligentsia were faced with a similar challenge of re-drawing and revaluating their positions. For Poles, however, the geopolitical context of such revisions was rather different in the aftermath of national defeats. In the confluence of the positivist injunction of organic work at the grassroots, struggles for national sovereignty and re-building of the Polish statehood, the intelligentsia had leadership in these pursuits assigned to them. The discussions unfolding today seem to resemble the debates rife in the early years of the communist rule in Poland, which heralded the wrestling of the old and the new spirits, with all impending changes betokened in the unprecedented upward mobility of workers and peasants. The period of mass-scale construction projects under the planned economy kindled hopes for social modernisation and offered to the creative minds incentives to critically interrogate the past. The revisory trend in social reflection is exemplified in Józef Chałasiński's sociological study *Społeczna genealogia inteligencji polskiej* (*Social genealogy of the Polish intelligentsia*) (1948). The book took on board the nobility heritage of the intelligentsia, condemning their pre-war attitudes, choices and conduct and pointing out vices to be eradicated. In his reckoning with the historical legacy and its utility, Chałasiński took an inimical position to the past: the socialist intelligentsia were to lead the state-coordinated reforms.

How important these issues are can be gleaned from the forever returning tide of public discussions. Like no other class in Poland, the intelligentsia constantly find themselves exposed to public judgment, summoned to account for tasks assigned to them, relied on for a critique of current developments and expected to formulate long-term forecasts. The debates are punctuated with diagnoses of crisis in the intelligentsia's mission, though, conspicuously, the criticism has always been levelled by the intelligentsia themselves. The crisis of the intelligentsia was identified as early as in 1910 by Stanisław Brzozowski, and writers and scholars have addressed the quandary repeatedly ever since. In the 1990s, the discussion was re-ignited, with the intelligentsia's role in the transition to the market economy being the fuel that kept it ablaze. That role must be considered against the backdrop of emergent new categories of the intelligentsia produced in the transformations of the occupational structure. New occupational positions signal the formation of the middle class, as was the case in late medieval England, where the gentry – the blueprint of the capitalist farmer – evolved from the mercantile-minded nobility, and a demand grew in towns for teachers, physicians, lawyers and moneymen.

The emergence of new occupations is a major aspect in the current transformations of the social structure in Poland. The process is accompanied by an increasing diversification between the intelligentsia, workers and peasants. Within the intelligentsia, a few categories can be distinguished, which I will discuss below. The most important development is the division into the old and the new intelligentsia. The former are still involved in the tasks ascribed to the intelligentsia in the times when the intelligents, as the common phrase went, were able to stir their environment to action and "turn every spot they were hurled into by fate and history into an outpost." The latter is comprised of specialists resembling Western-style professionals rather than champions of the traditional ethos. Given Poland's impending accession to the European Union, the question is whether a populous group in occupations united by a shared ideology will survive or cede ground to specialists. Are intellectuals, preachers and "café politicians" going to be replaced by public-relations, marketing and human-resources experts? Based on this division, we will be able to examine two currently fashionable theses, namely that the intelligentsia are becoming extinct and that the intelligentsia is disintegrating, which will eventually cause its complete disappearance.

The Managerial Intelligentsia

The upper layers of the intelligentsia are made up by senior managers, whose distinct position is defined by professional expertise combined with an executive authority within firms, organisations and state administration. In broad lines, the term "manager" designates here directors of private and public-sector companies. The basic reason why senior managerial staff are counted among the intelligentsia is that recruitment to the category is based, among others, on higher education credentials. But it is not the only reason. Managers and executives resemble the intelligentsia also in social status, especially in the material standard of living, attitudes and life styles.

Managers are thus the intelligentsia members holding positions of power in business organisations, holdings, joint stock companies, etc. – they are chairpersons, deputy chairpersons, board members and department managers for shipment, human resources, accounting, and the like. What are they actually – the intelligentsia or business people? The supervisory positions are usually associated with ownership in a broad sense of the term. People who have a sufficient shareholding or a formal deed title are capable of running the company more like owners than like managers, depending on which of these roles prevails. The balance between the two roles is not quite settled, and it is debatable whether directors-and-owners in one should be counted among managerial staff or whether, perhaps, they belong to the big-business world. Bill Gates or, in Poland, Sobiesław Zasada and Jan Kulczyk are an excellent case in point: they are both owners and corporate CEOs, members of boards of directors, etc. This problem of double class membership, unresolved in analytical reflection yet (Roemer 1982; Wright 1996), concerns not only managers, but also, for example, self-employed peasants hired at the same time as bricklayers.

The former managers of state-owned enterprises, who in the 1990s turned business executives in the market economy, were faced with a challenge of running the companies and developing business strategies freely, i.e. independently of the state-issued directives. The disbanding of huge state-owned consortiums and central managements eliminated a host of directors and created a gap which was filled by concern chairmen, financial specialists and managers with MBA or BA degrees from Columbia, Berkeley and London School of Economics. Some of them started their careers in renowned companies abroad, and others did internships in the Polish branches of such multinationals as Neumann Group, Ernst & Young or Arthur Andersen. Initially customer advisers, specialists or chairman assistants, they climbed the promotion ladder to become directors for logistics or marketing and members of management boards.

The dismantling of the mentality and working habits moulded by the former system is a complex and arduous process. And it is best encouraged by the financial incentives. Senior managerial positions are, by far, unparalleled in securing conspicuously high incomes as confirmed by a recent nationwide survey (Domański 2000a). The market research commissioned by the daily *Rzeczpospolita* (2001) and carried out by Hewitt Associates in 2000 shows that the average monthly income of directors in production companies based on the Polish capital approximated gross PLN 10,000 while the average income for entire Poland, according to the Central Statistical Office data, stood at PLN 1,700. In the Warsaw-based firms included in the survey, 75% of directors in production companies earned above PLN 8,000 a month, and in other regions of Poland their incomes did not drop below PLN 5,500. The difference is caused, among others, by the highest living costs and a considerable demand for managerial staff in the business-studded capital, where multiple companies compete for the best specialists, enticing them with financial rewards.

CEOs are indisputable leaders in earnings. In foreign-capital companies the payroll differences are bigger than in Polish companies; on the whole, earnings are more diversified and higher in the former. Every fourth chairman or managing director in companies with foreign capital outside Warsaw made above PLN 255,000 a year, while in Warsaw the figure stood at above PLN 477,000. And we should remember that the maximum salary (thirty times the national average salary) for directors in companies covered by the so-called salary-cap act (i.e. those where the State Treasury owned a major share) was expected to slightly top 54,000 PLN in 2001. This is merely a shade of a real income gap as compared with Western companies. According to an international study conducted in 1991, members of management boards in America earned 85 times as much as an average worker, in Britain 35 times as much, and in Germany 25 times as much. In 1988, Lawrence Rawl, director of Exxon, made $5.5 million (Hampden-Turner and Trompenaars 1998: 59).

If the remuneration offered represents a demand for particular occupations, financial, marketing, human resources and IT specialists were the relatively most sought-after experts at the threshold of the second decade of capitalism. For example, the total monthly salary of a financial director in Warsaw oscillated between gross PLN 11,000 and 26,000, with the figure in foreign capital companies topping the national average by 17%. A marketing director could make between PLN 5,600 and 13,700; in this case, salaries in foreign marketing companies exceeded the Polish average by 98%.

The situation of senior managerial staff exemplifies the principle of the capitalist labour market – that personal value is determined by the level of income. On the one hand, the dominance of economic relations simplifies and impoverishes human relationships, but, on the other, it clarifies the intricate mechanisms of conversion of individual capitals into social standing. Fully engrossed in their company's business, directors regard the income level as a measure of utility and personal achievement. The financial hierarchy, the most palpable and most commonly upheld of all hierarchies, forms a universal point of reference for various motivations and incentives. A common instrument in recruiting demanded specialists is an offer of extra benefits. According to the Hewitt Associates survey (which involved 48 companies) cited above, directors of big companies are given company cars to use at will not only for company business. Higher managerial staff have their travel expenses reimbursed without inquiring into particulars of the journey and fuel repaid irrespective of mileage. Mobile phones and computers are standard equipment made available to directors also for private use by every second Warsaw-based company and one in three companies outside Warsaw. Every other company in the capital offers its directors a life insurance package of their choice. More exclusive benefits include services of housemaids and drivers, business class flights and funding of children's education. The non-financial rewards are likely to increase as suggested by observations in the West, where such benefits make up a greater share in the overall reward package than in Poland.

The Civil Service

The professional civil service came into being as a result of modernisation processes which embraced all state offices. In the mid-19th century, as governments were gradually assuming responsibility for communication, transportation, education and welfare, the scant staff of the bureaucratic apparatus, the judiciary, the diplomatic service and other governmental agencies in Western Europe were confronted with a growing volume of tasks. The previous practice of inheriting or buying offices was abandoned for a new human resources policy in which recruitment and promotion rules were brought into alignment with the rationalities dictated by the market forces.

England was the cradle of the civil service. The civil service germinated in the 1860s, when the Northcote-Trevelyan Commission, appointed by the government in 1860, submitted a series of legislation projects to the Parliament (Northcote and Trevelyan authored the report). Following the Commission's recommendations, the Gladstone cabinet in a sweep of liberal, reformatory passion instituted a competition procedure as the basic recruitment form for civil servants and made promotion contingent upon the objective criteria of competence. These changes were soon followed by the abolition of the sale of officer commissions. As a result, the ministerial buildings in the Whitehall started swarming with new civil servants single-mindedly dedicated to technical efficiency and impartiality in dealing with cases. The civil service corps was founded upon the cornerstone of political neutrality, which gave rise to a new occupational category ousting the former "gentleman's career" pattern, which privileged aristocracy and perpetuated the medieval patronage system.

The determination of the reformers was matched by the vehemence of the critics. Opining that "[t]here are places in life which can hardly be well filled except by 'Gentlemen,'" Anthony Trollope (1978: 34) articulated a by no means uncommon sentiment. As late as in 1930, the Association of First Division Civil Servants cautioned in a statement submitted to the Royal Commission on Civil Service that the civil service no longer enjoyed the highest prestige it had once had and was no guarantee of proper status, which, the Association believed, had diminished its appeal and lessened the quality of its ranks (Guttsman 1969: 262).

Scarcity of the civil service in Poland is a direct effect of the historical conjuncture dating back to the partition period of 1795-1918. With no sovereign statehood, the Polish intelligentsia from the very outset worked toward promoting the idea of the supremacy of the nation, which hampered the development of civic consciousness and respect for the legal norms instituted by the state authority. The discriminatory policies implemented by Prussia and Russia, two of the partitioning powers, deprived Poles of meaningful careers opportunities in the state administration, not to mention that such pursuits anyway smacked of ignoble, treacherous collaboration with the enemy. Polish society also resented the occupiers' law. Legislative thinking on a daily basis was practised in conspiracy, and reverence for the underground state structures was inculcated. While Poles nurtured conspiratorial sentiments, Western democracies painstakingly strove to build effective government administration and fostered trust in the authorities. The British civil servants spared no effort in their proud commitment to furthering the imperial cause.

Poland used these models in the 1990s to create its own civil service practically from scratch. The most renowned school whose graduates feed the ranks of the civil service is École Nationale d'Administration, which trains senior officials in France. Each year thousands of candidates take competitive examinations to be eligible for admission to ENA. The school's fundamental premise holds that the graduates are to be apolitical functionaries with a thorough understanding of the state affairs, who will warrant the stability of the state in any political configuration regardless of what political party may be in power. The students are taught solving governance-related problems in territorial administration, economic decision-making, public affairs management, budget and fiscal issues, diplomacy and international contacts. *Les énarques*, i.e. the ENA graduates, choose their first positions depending on their place in the final ranking. How effectively this system works can be seen in the graduate statistics: in 2000, about 83% of the

ENA alumni worked in administration and public enterprises, 37 out of 577 current members of the National Assembly graduated from ENA, as did 12 out of 321 senators and 9 out of 27 ministers. Two former presidents, Jacques Chirac and Valéry Giscard d'Estaing, also studied at ENA.

ENA is a model which Poland seeks to emulate. Polish senior officials are educated in Krajowa Szkoła Administracji Publicznej (National School of Public Administration) – KSAP – founded in 1991. Its history so short, KSAP has not yet been able to produce a prime minister. KSAP study cycles take twenty months, including internships in Poland and abroad. Eligible candidates to full-time programmes must be MA degree holders aged below 32. So far, the number of applicants for each study place available oscillated between 4.2 and 8.4 applicants. Over the 10 years since the school's foundation, 396 students have graduated from KSAP, completing either full-time programmes or upgrading courses for officials already working in state administration.

How can the intelligentsia be turned into the middle class? The short history of KSAP would seem to imply that the process of building a competence-based state administration is already underway. The applications submitted to the school are at least twice as many as the number of possible admissions. The data suggest that the graduates are sought mainly by the central state institutions: in 2000, there were 57 KSAP graduates among directors and deputy-directors of departments in governmental offices and ministries. Earlier graduates took such positions as Head of the Civil Service, Head of the National Civil Defence, Chief of the Custom Service and general directors of many central offices. Press reports often dwell on how closely-knit the civil service corps is due to tight bonding among the KSAP graduates, whom journalists called "ksapers," which admittedly sounds nearly as emphatic as *les énarques*. *Rzeczpospolita* has reported that "ksapers scrupulously guard their apolitical stance. They continue to be a homogeneous group engaged in mutual communication. The school's annals have recorded only one graduate who joined a political party." The decision, as we learn from the uplifting passage, was rather coldly received (Gestern 2000).

Encouraged by these facts suggestive of institutionalisation of new careers, we could speculate that the civil service is a breeding ground of pragmatically-minded experts. However, such hypotheses are belied by opposite developments, especially in the standards of political neutrality, a determinant of the new ethos. All governments after 1989 sought to reform administration and safeguard senior administrative offices from becoming the "spoils of war" seized by the election-winning party. To accomplish this feat, one condition had to be met: the civil service corps needed to be disassociated from the political system. This, however, was not to be: a noble-minded vision invariably fell into pieces after each consecutive parliamentary election. Political analysts observe that public administration has been effectively appropriated by political parties, and it is not without a reason that the public opinion views it as a nest of malfeasance. The law on the civil service came into force under the coalition government of the post-communist Democratic Left Alliance and the Polish Peasant Party (Polskie Stronnictwo Ludowe), yet throughout the period in power (1993-1997) they did not eschew the practice of appointing and promoting officials based on their political affiliation.

Following the Western models, KSAP releases rankings of its graduates in order to channel the best students into the highest posts. Nevertheless, so far only 20 out of about 600 management-level positions in central administration have been filled based on the competition procedure in force. The law stipulates that recruitment through competition applies to all public administration posts below ministerial advisors, starting with general directors – the highest appointed officials, who should have a decisive influence on the administrative work of their subordinates. In fact, the law repeatedly fails in confrontation with practice as party-anchored policy-makers often circumvent apolitical directors and pass their commands directly to the junior staff. It seems, thus, that the sphere theoretically entrusted to civil servants is still a playground of politicians, who indulge in their games across its hierarchies.

The Professions

The apocalyptic predictions of the demise of the intelligentsia may well be an exercise in fashionable revisionism or an effect of predilection for airing spectacular views. Resisting such pessimism, we will look into the development of another category, namely the professions. Prospects for the formation of this category are a key factor in our discussion of the middle class, yet they are still empirically unclear. I will thus attempt to establish to what extent part of the intelligentsia can indeed be replaced by the professions of the Anglo-American type.

In very broad lines, two main attributes of the intelligentsia are university education and high-status occupational positions consequent upon it. This rudimentary description does not explain much, especially when we try to understand why the intelligentsia, and not any other social class, were persistently the driving force of radical transformations at the recent historical turning points. Some argue that it was the case because the intelligentsia erected service to society into an ethical injunction (Pipes 1990). The intelligents are not simply educated individuals preoccupied with their own good and personal achievement, but first and foremost people committed to a public cause whether they draft expert reports or devise strategies aimed to amend the social system and the state. Another argument advanced by Pipes is that the intelligentsia are customarily engaged in opposition to the state authorities. The intelligentsia enter the stage whenever the public opinion disagrees with the government, which obviously does not stop the intelligentsia from playing a self-appointed mouthpiece of the masses.

The criteria specified by Pipes are met by the Polish intelligentsia with a specific, historically conditioned local twist. Whereas in other countries the authorities and intellectuals clashed over conflicting class interests, with the latter pitting their own existential values and unfulfilled ambitions against governmental rules, in Poland the struggle focused on the national liberation. The Russian intellectuals fought against *samoderzhavie* (tsarist autocracy) and promulgated liberation of the people, the working class and the peasantry. In the times of the Popular Front of the 1930s, the French intellectuals, leaders of the West-European left, fought against the decadent bourgeoisie and the capitalist system. Importantly, the radical French intellectuals stepped to the fore at the end of the 19th century, consolidating their ranks in a propagandist campaign in defence of captain Alfred Dreyfus, who had been convicted for treason. Prominent public figures, such as Émile Zola, upheld universalist principles against the conservative values and vocally remonstrated against sacrificing Dreyfus for the sake of the French Army's honour or *raison d'État*. After Dreyfus was convicted to long-term imprisonment, politicians and the officer corps protested against revoking the unjust sentence, which gesture would allegedly undercut the credibility of the French state. Zola's famous open letter *J'accuse*, published on 13 January 1898 in the daily *L'Aurore*, was a seminal event also because it ushered the term "an intellectual" into colloquial language.

If persisting in opposition to the establishment speaks of indefatigability, the intellectuals have definitely gloried in it as in a special privilege. In each society, there are a handful of "defiant" critics who, gifted with a "professional" skill of resenting the authorities, revel in dissent. In Poland, another stereotypical role model was provided by an enlightened, dutiful, self-sacrificial social activist, who educated the lower social strata and guided the nation. The admirable image had also its less appealing facets, vividly outlined in Ignacy Daszyński's memoirs (1957: 64-65). In the 1890s, "an intelligent-socialist was a candidate for an unadorned starveling. Graduating from university, he would either become a clerk or join the so-called liberal professions as a lawyer or a physician [...]. And a 'liberal' professional had to scrape for every penny."

In this way, a group of educated, but mostly poor professionals emerged, having rather vague prospects of actually working in their jobs and steeped in the Polish "impossibility" complex. In fact, the intelligentsia had the ethos of social activism ascribed to them not only in Poland, as shown by Jerzy Jedlicki (2000), yet the Polish intelligentsia were compelled to live it and breathe it far longer under the pressure of communism with its contrived abstraction-informed doctrine. Without affecting the occupational roles as such, this effectively thwarted the development of pragmatist attitudes dedicated to improving the education system, health care, legislation and the judiciary.

The first decade of the transition to a market society has amply shown that no myth poses an insurmountable barrier. The intelligentsia have split into two categories, each pledging allegiance to a different logic. One of them, associated mainly with the state-funded institutions, cherishes the legacy of the welfare budget logic while the other, associated predominantly with the market sector, prioritises measurable delivery and outcomes.

Professionalisation of the intelligentsia is institutionally underpinned by the development of the education system and occupational training. At the beginning of 2000, there were 92 state universities, 135 non-public, entirely tuition-based universities and 50 higher vocational colleges (14 thereof non-public), which offered B.A. degrees or, equivalent, engineer certifications. Altogether, thus, toward the end of the first decade of the transformation, higher education was provided by 277 schools, the figure covering branch departments, satellite campuses, military schools and schools founded by the Ministry of the Interior. This represented an unprecedented growth of the higher education system, with a fourfold increase in the number of students and a rise of the scholarisation index (the ratio of students to the total population in the 19-24 age group) from 13% to 33.5% between 1989 and 1999. This was primarily an effect of an astounding proliferation of non-public universities, which educated nearly one third of young people, as well as of an expansion of extra-mural study programmes, which, though more easily accessible, offered far lower quality education than full-time degrees. Also, studying abroad became a more widely available educational option. Foreigners can study in Germany for free; in the USA foreign students do pay tuition, but many schools offer discounts of various kinds; in England scholarships can be obtained with relative ease; and in France state-run universities offer education free of charge. It is mandatory for eligible candidates to know a corresponding foreign language with the degree of proficiency certified by relevant examinations.

Young experts in telecommunications, electronics, IT and other fast developing industries can take advantage of job fairs in Poland and abroad to get in touch with prospective employers. Intech, a trade fair organised by Fairtile in Poznan twice in 2000, turned out a very successful event. While in Poland it was perhaps somewhat of a novelty, Berlin's job fair organised by London-based recruitment company Disco International is already long established and traditionally very well attended. In its 12 editions so far, Eurotech Career Forum, as it is officially known, has hosted more than 800 companies and 50 thousand visitors. Job-seekers talk with representatives of employers, submit their resumes and perform their first job interviews. As the organisers emphasise, the fair offers a unique opportunity to meet employers in person, which is not something that employment agencies can provide (an argument which salvages the sense of local colour apparently long evacuated from market transactions). Western employers inspect the skills of candidates from Eastern Europe, with lower labour cost put on the latter's credit side, but with poor knowledge of foreign languages and employability constrained by labour legislation as their importunate liabilities (the present study covers the period from before Poland's accession to the European Union). Patently, the West has lost much of the powerful grip it used to exert on Poles travelling abroad in the past. The young go abroad to find out about the ways of the world and make contacts. In most cases, they plan to stay away a few years at the most to acquire occupational experience and develop expertise to be later used in Poland.

Over these few recent years, renowned companies have implemented active policies of young staff recruitment and development. International consultants and insurers, such as Arthur Andersen, PricewaterhouseCoopers or Nationale Nederlanden, recruit from among graduate students without actually stipulating any particular school type, though graduate rankings are a factor in the process. The selection involves a multi-stage procedure: preliminary selection based on CV's and letters of motivation is followed by a series of interviews in which analytical thinking, team-working skills and problem-solving aptitudes are tested.

Professionalisation entails also constant upgrading of skills in specialised training schemes and courses. First lists of the most successful training companies and their financial results were released in the first half of 2000. According to them, the turnover of 46 leading companies exceeded PLN 1,000,000 (i.e. $250,000). Besides specialised companies offering training in human resources management, communication, business skills and negotiations, there were also firms which organised courses in computer skills, certification, real estate trading, logistics, health and safety, etc. The rapidly growing training market has learnt to recognise emerging trends, identify new challenges and respond flex-ibly. For example, 1999-2000 saw many courses in amended labour legislation, and the year 2001 witnessed them replaced by courses in revisions to the com-mercial code.

What are the implications of these developments? Like in Western countries, a specialised degree should entail a range of advantages, such as greater pro-motion opportunities and comfortable income. Indeed, such expectations are to some extent substantiated by the findings of an international survey of the managerial intelligentsia carried out in October 1999. In 17 countries, the re-spondents were asked whether, in their opinion, additional education, such as MBA programmes, increased chances of employment. In Poland, 80% of the 233 respondents answered that it did, and a nearly identical proportion (almost 80%) highly assessed the utility of skill-upgrading and qualification-improving courses (Suchar 2000).

New occupational roles have somewhat invalidated the traditional position and the ethos of the intelligentsia. Several examples force a realisation that pro-fessionals employed in newly emergent jobs cannot be the same social stratum that the intelligentsia historically used to be. Let us take, for example, experts of public relations, defined as the occupational roles whose responsibilities involve creating and sustaining advantageous relationships between an organisation and the groups on which its success and failure depend. The aim of public relations is to build a desirable image of the company by disseminating reliable infor-mation about it and, thereby, winning the customers' trust and sustaining their interest. In seeking to create the company's favourable image, PR experts target both its employees and the public at large – they work toward preventing or solv-ing employee-management conflicts, collaborate closely with the media, arrange sponsoring campaigns, organise social and "consciousness-raising" events and engage in lobbying. Though laymen sometimes mistake image-creation for com-mon advertising, the public relation specialists see the subtle differences between the two as all important in delimiting their profession. The Polish PR Association founded in 1994 assembled around 150 members. According to the data from 1997 (Czarnowski 1997), PR services were offered by at least 200 companies, with the figure not including freelance PR practitioners.

The commercialisation of the intelligentsia is also visible in professionalisation of advertising. Advertising is defined as a professional strategy for management of intangible assets geared toward generating and conveying information which distinguishes the company vis-à-vis its competitors. Effectiveness of advertis-ing in its early stage depends on whether the potential customers recognise its utility. Success is measured not by the originality of the idea, unusually creative though it might be, but by verifiable, practical outcomes. According to experts, the key to success lies in the planning of an advertising campaign and mastering the technicalities involved in launching it in the mass media. Particular activities comprised in the overall plan are performed by small task-focused teams. Big advertising agencies already offer a full range of specialised services, from graphic design to channelling contacts with the media. Yet the heart of an advertising agency beats in its creative department, where highly imaginative individuals must reconcile aspirations to originality with pragmatic requirements.

To comply with the new book-keeping standards, companies must have their financial records examined by auditors. The Accounting Act passed in Poland in 1994 makes audit mandatory for capital groups, banks, insurance companies, joint-stock companies, trust funds, investment funds and all companies with annual net proceeds above the stipulated level and year-average employment of 50 or more people. Only certified auditors are sanctioned to look into the finances of companies and report on them, which in principle resembles the authorised compulsory technical inspection of vehicles. Without being tax inspection staff, certified auditors – professionals with background in financial law and theoretical knowledge augmented by extensive on-the-job experience – investigate the audited companies' activities, culminating in an annual financial statement. Besides the inspection of records, audits in practice involve also advisory and consulting services which cover first of all taxation, book-keeping, insolvency and/ or liquidation proceedings and issuing of expert opinions and reports. Auditors are expected to observe the standard professional code of ethics: impartiality, confidentiality, unbiased attitude to the customer, dedication to competence and constant professional development. According to the ranking of audit companies published in 2000 by *Rzeczpospolita*, the top position was held by PricewaterhouseCoopers, which rendered services to 15% of the quoted companies in Poland.

Much suggests that an oversleeve-wearing book-keeper will soon be deposed by a certified accountant. The prototype of the occupation – the public chartered accountant – appeared in the mid-19th century in England in the aftermath of new legislation on commercial companies. In America, the profession emerged as a result of the income tax amendment passed by the Congress in 1909 and ratified in 1913. From then on, certified public accountants were supposed to guard the principles and practice of correct accounting. The growingly intricate taxation formalities made them indispensable to all companies, and the ruling of the newly instituted Board of Tax Appeals at the US federal government, which

stipulated that certified accountants were the only qualified corporate representatives, only boosted the already burgeoning demand for their services (Boorstin
1995: 212). In Poland, the Chartered Institute of Management Accountants was
set up in July 2000 with a basic aim to provide professional training of certified
accounting staff. According to foreign experts, Polish accountants meet the demands of revenue offices and the Social Insurance Institution (ZUS); however,
they do not have adequate competence to draft periodical reports in ways which
could facilitate decision-making at various corporate levels. Adjusting accountants' capabilities to Western business operation models is a prerequisite to a closer intertwining of book-keeping, planning, monitoring and financial strategies
designing in companies.

The Intelligentsia in the Budget Sector

The intelligentsia that evolved under the communist system enjoyed no lesser
esteem than pre-war attorneys, academic luminaries or provincial apothecaries –
ultimate arbiters in matters of social life, exponents of correctness and guard-
ians of the only right views. The lower classes were always impressed by the
intelligentsia's unquestioned cultural erudition and accomplishments, unaffect-
ed bearing and what was considered conversational ease.

The severance of ties with the past after the war did not alter those sentiments, and the intelligentsia continued as a symbol of esoteric nobility without
a coat-of-arms. The communist system dismantled, however, the cherished monopoly which the intelligentsia had held as a demiurge of social pedagogy and
demolished its chances for genuine professionalism. Some of the intelligentsia
re-captured these chances at the onset of the market economy in the 1990s. But
a good part of the intelligentsia, popularly referred to as "the budget-sector intelligentsia," are heirs to the group formed under the former regime. This category
finds itself dangling in-between two epochs. It includes engineers in state-run
enterprises, teachers in public schools and a vast group of clerical staff working
in administration, who all live on 70-80% of what the intelligentsia employed in
private companies earn and drudge along at their desks just to make it to retire-
ment. Of course, this is a generalised remark, basically concerning the mean
figures. Notably, the budget sector was regarded in the 1990s as an oasis for the
working class categories as it offered them, on the average, higher wages than the
private sector did. In contrast, the intelligentsia fared better in private companies
(Domański 1997). In their attitudes to life, the intelligentsia employed in the
budget-funded firms often combine sore loser moods, elitist phobias and pre-
tensions to high status. Ideologically lukewarm, they are relegated to the margin

of changes, which likens them to anonymous hosts of Western "white collars" devoid of any explicit views. Their passivity and frustration make them into perfectly manipulable puppets manoeuvred by politicians whenever general election is coming.

To proclaim a decay of the intelligentsia is a gross oversimplification as it overlooks crucial differences between an engineer in a factory on the verge of bankruptcy and a skilful financier, a consultant or a marketing specialist. In fact, even the intelligentsia working in the public sector still stands as the best candidate to bet one's money on in a race toward middle-class membership, as, untypically, its openness to change implies. Moving place of residence frequently is a distinct feature of the American life style. The American labour market offers many advantageous opportunities and, at the same time, a company's bankruptcy is hardly a life-shattering disaster for its employees, unlike it tends to be in Poland. Whenever the economy slips down the slope, everybody can expect being summoned to the management room and handed a lay-off letter. Hence, experienced specialists in branches valued by the market send around their resumes and negotiate new jobs with prospective employers in advance, which shortens unemployment stints. A Bostonian hardly hesitates to jump on a plane and relocate to Denver, Colorado, (3 hours away) for, likely, the next 1-2 years until a new opportunity presents itself.

This is not yet routine in Poland, but, as compared with the other categories, the intelligentsia is the most mobile social class, which is shown by the data on mobility throughout occupational career. According to the findings of a national survey in 1998, the intelligentsia changed place of residence 2.7 times on the average, mid-ranked administrative staff 2.4 times, lower clerical workers 1.9 times and business owners 2.3 times, while the figures for various worker categories oscillated between 1.5 and 1.7, and stood at 1.6 for farmers, who were certainly at the lowest.

These optimistic findings do not alleviate the predicament faced by all the department heads, office clerks and accountants whose work is popularly associated with the unproductive tedium of paper-scribbling and tea-drinking. In enacting new occupational roles, the older generation find themselves rebounding once and again from a stone-wall of habits inculcated by working for the old-style state institutions. In chronological terms, age is a decisive criterion for the intelligentsia working in the old-style state institutions as the coming twenty years will witness their gradual disappearance. This does not mean, of course, that when they finally leave the stage, the intelligentsia will vanish altogether. Such occupational category functions quite successfully in all Western societies because the contemporary capitalist system is largely based on state capitalism.

Conclusion

Probably, hardly any of occupational categories included in the broad class of "the intelligentsia" resisted the pressures of the market transformations. Only the intelligentsia in the budget sector seem to be still steeped in the modes of old, but their days are counted, and their apparently solid presence is but an already subsiding momentum effect. The complex processes in which the old intelligentsia is being converted into the new one, comprised of occupations corresponding to the Anglo-American new middle class, are best observable in another two categories.

One of them includes writers, artists, composers, musicians, filmmakers and actors. The quandary that haunts the creative intelligentsia is how to preserve the classic artistic canons and, at the same time, meet commercial requirements. Under the previous system, the creative milieus particularly valued independence from the authorities, upheld moral imperatives and were commended for dissidence or opposition to the regime in the name of true values and ideals. Commercialisation, however, has wreaked havoc in those hierarchies. Artists and authors have found themselves in an awkward situation of having their roles turned upside down without knowing when and how exactly it came to pass other than by a magic trick played by some conjurer. The trick was actually that the audience seats were taken by wealthy clients. If an artist reaps applause for professionalism now, we can safely surmise that what is being praised is adaptability to the market mechanisms. A priest of pure form, a rebel, a bohemian are neither alluring nor feasible roles if profit is all important, comfortable life a priority and remaining popular an imperative.

Such developments imply a handful of conclusions. Firstly, if once concessions had to be made to the communist regime, they are now demanded by the market. In other words, the difference between the old system and the new one boils down to swopping the old constraints for the new rigours: no longer used and shielded by the state, the creative intelligentsia have been seized and subordinated by demanding customers and companies. Secondly, artists, who need acclaim just as much as air, have been cajoled into philistine postures, gracing prestigious award ceremonies and frequenting banquets where ostentatious self-satisfaction and cool are requisite. Thirdly, to make a living by trading art one must abandon the aspirations of an adamant champion of values. Clerical autonomy, it seems, is a utopian fantasy in any social system.

The other subcategory of the new middle class is made up of university professors. A prototype of a genuine profession, the academic teacher came into being alongside the medical doctor, the lawyer and the priest in the late Middle Ages. In developed capitalist economies, children's education determines daily schedules and sets the rhythm of life in middle-class families. In planning the day, parents must take into account the timetable of transporting children to school and back home as well as the extra-mural activities in which parental presence is expected. The choice of school, from early education facilities up to college, involves a well-studied strategy devised with a future career in mind and implemented from the child's early age on. In the United States, where that system has been perfected beyond compare, universities are an inseparable part of local landscapes, the space punctuated with characteristic green, tree-studded areas where modern buildings are interlaced with medievalised college architecture.

Education industry, which caters to the masses, enforces professionalisation. Lecturers are evaluated for research outcomes on the basis of submissions accepted by journals with rejection rates of 90%. The labour market is highly competitive with a few hundred candidates applying for one vacancy advertised in an open competition. But on the credit side of things, renowned tenured professors at the richest universities, such as Harvard or Yale, make $300,000 a year, while the average salary in permanent jobs ranges between $50,000 and $100,000. In Poland, however, professional rankings are hardly applicable because in terms of academic positions the higher education market is not competitive, and to receive three applications for one job opening would make a faculty proud. In the 1990s, higher education expanded unprecedentedly as far as the number of schools and students is concerned, but the constantly growing demand was met by the staff already in place. For lecturers, working in multiple jobs has become a routine solution, to the detriment of the teaching and research quality.

Perennial debates on whether the intelligentsia are yet around seem to suggest that they are still crucial in meeting social needs. An economically backward country, Poland essentially needed a cultural elite, self-appointed keepers of the supreme values, to express public desires and provide spirituals leadership. There is nothing to suggest that the intelligentsia's leading role in culture has been curtailed or their highest position in the prestige hierarchy undermined. Ever since research on occupational prestige began, university professors have invariably enjoyed the highest social esteem and the intelligentsia occupations have had an unbroken run in the top ten of the ranking (Domański 1999). The intelligentsia could become extinct only in a society without history. Consequently, the question whether the intelligentsia still exist should be reformulated into who could possibly replace them, if at all.

Chapter VI: The Upper Class

> *What I want to know is; what is*
> *actually wrong with an elite, for*
> *God's sake?*
>
> Charles, Prince of Wales

Looking for the middle class, we should not lose track of a related category, that is, the upper class, which is an immanent part of the hierarchical division into the upper, middle and lower class. In Anglo-American culture, the division has become the basic framework for organising the social hierarchy. In Western countries, the terms "upper," "middle" and "lower" have been commonly used in colloquial language for a few hundred years now, and the social sciences made them part of coherent theories corroborated by empirical research.

The distinction into "upper," "middle" and "lower" classes was systematically investigated by William Lloyd Warner, a prominent socio-anthropologist who initiated comprehensive research on American local communities. Starting their empirical project in the 1930s, W.L. Warner and his team produced a series of monograph studies, deemed (at that time) milestones of empirical sociology. The eponymous *Yankee City* and *Jonesville*, which appeared in the best know of these publications, are aliases of small towns in New England and the Mid-West, where the surveys were conducted, probing into practically all aspects of life, with a focus on paid labour, material living conditions, social relationships and everyday routines of the inhabitants.

Warner's team aimed mainly to capture more general principles and the social hierarchy of communal life (Warner 1949, Warner and Lunt 1941). On the basis of findings reported some years earlier by Helen and Robert Lynd (1929), Warner expected to find a dichotomous split into the upper and the lower class, which was the case in Middletown, as the Lynds called the town they had studied. However, he realised – to his own surprise, as he was to admit later – that the social structure of Yankee City and Jonesville was best conveyed as a gradation of six social categories or classes. For their inhabitants, the local elite was the old aristocracy – the wealthiest and most esteemed category called the "upper-upper class." Behind them ranked the new rich – owners of fortunes which had not acquired a noble lustre yet; and the lowest rung of the stratification ladder was taken by the underclass and the local poor. The top-to-bottom hierarchy included the following classes: "upper-upper," "lower-upper," "upper-middle," "lower-middle," "upper-lower" and "lower-lower." The terms, though bland enough in themselves, pointed to actual realities experienced by particular families and individuals.

Prospects for the development of the upper class in Poland are unclear. It does not figure in the public discourse on the future since (i) it is associated with elitism and smacks of snobbery, and (ii) it makes for a risky and thorny subject completely at odds both with political correctness and with egalitarian allegiances – a bequest of the previous system. Contrary to the middle class, which seems a focal point of reformist reconstruction projects, so far the reactivation of the upper class has not been considered as a serious option in the modernisation of the social structure.

What sense would the upper class make for Poland now? This can be answered very briefly: the social structure abhors a vacuum. Let's take the USA and its history. The American society did not know the genuine aristocracy – the country came into being in armed combat against European feudalism, promising a complete overhaul of social relationships. Extolling the republican values, Americans repudiated the idea of hereditary presidency and ruled against addressing George Washington as "His Highness," albeit after some heated arguments (Amory 1960: 61). Although those gestures seemed antimonarchic and unpropitious for the re-instating of the upper class, in 1783 The Society of the Cincinnati was formed (with Washington, Hamilton and Knox among the founding members), an event soon followed by the establishment of the First Families of Virginia. The subsequent decades saw the aristocracy revived in powerful and respected families, whose successors still set the tone in Boston, Philadelphia, Charleston and New York (with Long Island as their headquarters).

Is an upper class emerging in Polish society? To answer that question, we need to establish what the upper class exactly is in the West and then scrutinise it in specifically Polish contexts.

Attributes of the Upper Class: Wealth

The upper class is characterised by possession of wealth, great ancestral names, vast landed property, palaces, mansions, political influence and social prestige. This description would not spark objections in sociologists who study this issue, even within the Marxist paradigm, which is the most fiercely opposed to stratification theory identified with Western sociology. In the Marxian account, a part of the big-business could be seen as the equivalent of the upper class, though essentially the class structure in the capitalist world is based on the dyadic division into capitalists and workers. "The upper class" figured in Marxism, at best, as a backdrop against which to highlight the dynamics of conflicts. Let me digress that George Bernard Shaw (1884) said once that class polarisation involved, of old, two classes with "large appetites and no dinners at one extreme and large dinners and no appetite at the other." The literary panache of this line exudes the ideal of the equitable distribution of goods, eagerly advocated by Shaw, an active member of the Fabian Society, which flirted with Marxism.

Research carried out recently in Western countries and Japan implies that the upper class has a handful of universal characteristics. First of all, it is a relatively scant group which holds a considerable edge over the remaining categories in wealth and power. On the eve of World War Two, 75% of shares in all Japanese corporations belonged to 10 families, with 15% thereof possessed by the Mitsui family (Morikawa 1992). In the United States, the Rockefeller family in its halcyon days owned more than the Mitsui but never equalled their powerful influence on the domestic economy. Since 1918, *Forbes Magazine* has been publishing lists of America's richest people based on tax statements, inheritance tax records and property value estimates. The 1996 list included owners of fortunes in excess of one billion dollars.

Table 16: The richest Americans in the self-made man category

Name, company (industry)	Estimated worth in $ billions
William Gates (Microsoft)	18.5
Warren Buffet (investing)	15.0
Paul Allen (Microsoft)	7.5
John Kluge (Metromedia)	7.2
Lawrence Ellison (Oracle)	6.0
Phillip Knight (Nike)	5.3
Robert Perellman (buyouts)	4.0
Steven Ballner (Microsoft)	3.7
Gordon Moore (Intel)	3.7
Kirk Kerkovan (investing)	3.4
Summer Stone (Viacom)	3.4
Ross Perot (EDS)	3.3
Richard de Vos (Amway)	3.2
William Hewlett (H-P)	2.9
Ian Hutsman (chemicals)	2.5

Name, company (industry)	Estimated worth in $ billions
George Soros (fund management)	2.5
Marvin Davis (oil)	2.2
Ted Turner (media)	2.1

Source: Hacker 1998, p. 96.

Table 16 includes the names of the richest US citizens classified as self-made men, that is, those who are the makers of their own success, according to *Forbes*. Bill Gates, the leader of the ranking, owned estimated $18.5 billion, and Ted Turner, a media mogul closing the list, had $2.1 billion worth of fortune, only a bit shy of GDP of Central African republics, such as Congo, for example. Together with Sumner Stone and John Kluge (also featuring in the list), Turner represented the expansive cutting-edge companies, including TV, film studios, press, publishing and video stores.

The data in Table 17 illustrate the continuity of great fortunes of America's twenty richest families. As some of them were founded in the early 19th century, they can be viewed as structurally consolidated, to a degree at least, representatives of the upper class. The Walton family from the very top of the hierarchy has accumulated $24.8 billion worth of fortune. Du Pont ($13.9 billion), the oldest of the companies listed, has been in operation since 1802. The Gund family, which owns $2.1 billion and takes the bottom position in the list, has been involved in real estate and food business since 1919. Clearly, the history of the business elite stretches over centuries.

Table 17: America's twenty wealthiest families in 1996

Name, company (industry)	Founded in	Estimated worth (in $billions)
Walton (retailing)	1902	24.8
Du Pont (chemicals)	1802	13.9
Mars (candy)	1911	12.0
Rockefeller (oil)	1870	9.9
Newhouse (publishing)	1922	9.0
Haas (jeans)	1873	8.6
Bass (oils)	1930s	8.1
Cox (newspapers)	1898	8.0
Cargill (grain)	1865	7.9

Name, company (industry)	Founded in	Estimated worth (in $billions)
Dorrance (foods)	1876	7.7
Pritzker (finance)	1902	6.0
Mellon (banking)	1869	5.8
Lauder (cosmetics)	1946	4.1
Scripps (newspapers)	1870s	3.6
Upjohns (pharmaceutical)	1885	3.2
Ziff (publishing)	1927	3.0
Smith (machinery)	1889	2.8
Davis (groceries)	1925	2.3
Chandler (newspapers)	1894	2.1
Gund (food, real estate)	1919	2.1

Source: Hacker 1998, p. 95.

The distance between the upper class and the middle class is measured in billions and hundreds of millions. These figures are a multiple of what an average American owns, still having his needs met and enjoying a pleasant life. In the USA with the population of 270 million, 49.3% of corporate stock was owned by 0.5% of the wealthiest individuals in the 1990s, and 1% of the richest Americas owned 56.5% thereof (Kerbo 1996: 168). The *Forbes* lists identify the genuine elite of wealth, although how many billionaires there are in America actually is rather difficult to pinpoint with any precision because the US law prohibits inspecting personal bank accounts. The information based on tax statements, though reliable, is incomplete because they do not represent all sources of wealth. According to the estimates, in 1994 about 68,000 American citizens had incomes of at least $1 million. The average income in that group came to $2,483,000, with 87% reporting that their income stemmed from salaried work, and 19% – from proceeds from their own business (Hacker 1998: 73). It should be added that the capital of 15 million brought net returns of one million without any labour involved, and 40 million secured an annual income of 2.5 million.

In the UK, the royal family is at the apex of the rentier elite. In 1990, the members of the house of Windsor owned estimated £6.7 billion, which placed them on top of the wealthiest UK citizens, most of their wealth derived from land and real estate. The core of the wealth elite was made up by twenty wealthiest families, who held more than £50 million each. Duke of Westminster (4.2 billion) in the second place was followed by the families of Rausing (2 billion), Sainsbury

(1.8 billion), Weston (1.7 billion), Moores, Vestey and Getty (oil tycoons), owning more than £1,350 million each (Scott 1997: 83). The top twenty richest families included rentiers, big landowners and corporate entrepreneurs.

Attributes of the Upper Class: Authority and Power

Another attribute of the upper class is power: both economic power represented
mostly by owners and executives and political power based on taking part in
general governance. The impact of economic power is best judged by effects of
the upper-class activity since it is hardly possible to get an insight either into
political decision-making or into the processes in which decision-makers' will
translates into particular outcomes. One of the indicators of economic power
is the share of wealth held by the top 1% of the wealthiest people. In the USA,
this proportion stood at 56.5%. In England, the top 1% of the wealthiest families
held 21% of total wealth in 1986, which meant a twofold decrease as compared
with 1936 (53%). The economic dominance of the English elite has dropped by
half since the 1930s, the statistical effect due mainly to the exponential increase
in home ownership (Scott 1993) as the mortgage value of houses is included in
wealth statistics. With the larger percentage base, the concentration index fell
from 53% to 21%.

To what extent and in what ways these resources are controlled is determined
by decision-makers. Economic power, which means a capacity to actually control
individual wills, is executed through decision-making in which corporate executives and management board members have an ultimate say. According to early
research on the social origin of executive staff in America's twenty biggest industrial corporations, 54% of the executives had upper-class roots. In transportation, the percentage of senior managerial staff from the upper class stood at 53%;
in the 15 biggest banks – at 62%, and in the 15 largest insurance companies –
at 44% (Domhoff 1967). Apparently, no significant changes took place in recruitment mechanisms based on social origin in the course of time. In the 1990s,
research on the social origin of board members and senior managerial staff in
201 corporations showed that 44% of the 3572 respondents belonged to clubs
with exclusive upper class membership. These findings, according to Dye (1995),
proved the dominance of the upper class in corporate economic leadership.

The holders of such enormous wealth cannot be unconcerned with governmental policies which impact foreign trade or ways of handling inflation. The
upper class needs political power, and it is understandably more eager than other
social categories to acquire influence on investment policies, interest rates and
credit availability. How far the upper class can affect governmental decisions is

shown in studies which try to establish the rate of upper-class membership in governments, decision-making capacity and impact on appointments to key offices.

The data for the USA cover the presidency of Carter, Reagan and George Bush. Carter was a typical member of the middle class, yet he was, notably, recommended and supported in his run for presidency by the Trilateral Commission, an organisation assembling international corporate leaders, founded by David Rockefeller to further the interests of the American upper class. Prominent positions in the Carter administration were entrusted to, among others, Henry Kissinger and Zbigniew Brzeziński – the designees of the Council on Foreign Relations intimately associated with the Rockefeller family – and the president's other close collaborators rose to cabinet members via the same route (Dye 1978). While Carter was reckoned a spokesman for liberal partisans, Ronald Reagan – according to Domhoff (1983) – received backing from the conservative wing of the American upper class. Ten officials in the Reagan cabinet graduated from the elitist Ivy League universities, eleven had been presidents or management boards members in top corporations, and eight were members of the Council on Foreign Relations.

While Carter and Reagan were middle class, in George Bush America received a pure upper-class president, which was no exceptional event, actually, as John Fitzgerald Kennedy before him and Franklin Delano Roosevelt, earlier still, both stemmed from the upper class. President Kennedy's parents belonged to the exclusive and venerated elite of New England. Bush, largely helped by his father's wealth, studied at the elitist Philips Andover Academy and Yale, and started a very profitable oil business. In social terms, he also rubbed shoulders with the elite in clubs, such as the Bohemian Club, and prominent VIP organisations (Kerbo 1996).

Upper-class origin consistently improves and facilitates access to political power, as convincingly documented by Domhoff (1967: 97–99). His studies show that between 1932 and 1964 62%-63% of American Secretaries of State, Defence and Treasury stemmed from upper-class families. A longitudinal study carried out by Mintz (1975) scrutinised American cabinet members over a long time-span. Having analysed 205 political biographies from 1897-1972, he concluded that 66% of the government officials came from the upper class, and 54% of them were corporate executives or management board members in joint-stock companies.

Attributes of the Upper Class: Social Origin

Although wealth and power are crucial factors in recruitment to the highest positions, what matters the most for the upper class is social origin. New business tycoons, such as Bill Gates and George Soros, cannot be counted among the upper class. Similarly, although powerful politicians, Margaret Thatcher, François Mitterrand, Helmut Kohl or Bill Clinton were not upper class, either. After his presidency ended, Clinton would be paid $150,000 for guest lectures, while the sales of Hillary Clinton's memoirs brought her the record sum of $8 million, a figure higher than what Winston Churchill had made on his (putting inflation aside). A vast fortune, indeed, helps one get into the exclusive regions of the upper class, but it is by no means a passport to them. To qualify as upper class, individuals do not necessarily have to enjoy considerable wealth all the time, but they do have to boast a good lineage and family connections. These are true prerequisites of upper-class membership, which have a practical dimension to them after all – when business slackens, kin's help or an advantageous marriage are the surest way to bounce back.

The glamour of a good name arises from reverence bestowed on noble antiquity. The key factor lies in family history spanning over several generations. In all societies, the upper class is constituted by a group of families who are at the top of the prestige hierarchy and closely knit by friendship, familiarity and intermarriages. No other "class" is so firmly anchored in direct personal relationships, which help maintain its belief in exceptionality, distinct life style and group solidarity and identity.

The best starting point for the study of this issue is personal experience. A classic American analysis of the upper class concerns Philadelphia, the first capital of the United States (where the Declaration of Independence was signed), still regarded as an epitome of an aristocratic venue. The structural role of the upper class in Philadelphia was described in *Philadelphia Gentlemen* by Digby Baltzell (1958), an aristocratic sociologist and a member of the Philadelphia establishment himself. The book enumerates more attributes of the upper class than wealth and power. Discussing the role of family connections, Baltzell indicates that if the channels leading up to the middle class are, basically, open to everybody, the access to the upper class is a far more complicated venture. The emphasis on social roots turns the upper class into an original archetype in which the present merges with the time-honoured attributes of the nobility. It takes more to enter the upper class than simply passing exams, doing internship, graduating and getting a degree. It is not enough to just meet the formal criteria laid down for, say, a medical doctor or a civil servant. The upper class resembles the old aristocracy in exerting a political impact and having an impressive name, even though now most members of the upper class live off capital investments rather than landowning. The difference between the aristocracy and the upper class lies in that the latter is productive and exhibits remarkable activity. The traditional charges of moral decadence, indolence or sloth, which Europe's rich bourgeoisie hurled at the aristocracy in their contest for power, are hardly applicable to the upper class. The account would be incomplete without the dedication to the fair play code. Describing his generation, Baltzell (1991: 36) stresses that his peers abided by the rule of never disputing the umpire's calls when playing tennis.

Another trait of the upper class is exclusiveness. The American upper class treats the new rich as amoral gangsters and crooks rolled into one. In doing this, the old families seem wilfully oblivious of their own origins. It was a public secret that Joseph Kennedy, the president's father, the founder of the family fortune and a future US ambassador, made his fortune on illegal alcohol trafficking in the Prohibition era of the 1920s. In the American system, elite membership is institutionally symbolised by prestigious clubs. America's most esteemed all-male clubs are New Haven Lawn Club (New Haven), Rittenhouse (Philadelphia), Knickerbocker (New York), Boston (New Orleans) and the already mentioned Bohemian Club (San Francisco). The atmosphere which engulfs club meetings strengthens the sense of bonding, facilitates business dealings and fosters exchange of political views with implications far exceeding those of a polite conversation.

True, clubs were not invented for the upper class (the first clubs were set up in Paris and London in the 18th century to serve as meeting venues for rich burghers), but they turned out to be perfectly suited to fostering integration of exclusive milieus. Importantly, the upper class is a relatively scant group. If all American upper-class members were to convene, the gathering would not exceed the capacity of all existing clubs. In terms of self-organisation, the club is to the upper class what the factory is to big-industry workers, and a few dozen clubs provide an effective selection mechanism. Membership in the Bohemian Club is strictly invitational, and the admission procedure demands recommendations from two active members, an application with references from another five members, an interview with the membership committee and, finally, a ballot at the general gathering with all club members voting for or against the applicant (Domhoff 1974: 48–49).

Those who show off with ostentatious elitism are not welcome among the elites. Elite status is supposed to be communicated in registers, probably the most refined "accreditation" instrument ever invented in the history of class relations.

Registers inform about the upper class, providing the lists of names and families. They are published to let the general public know who actually is a member of the upper class. In the United States, the nationwide *Social Register* has been published since 1887 in parallel with several regional registers listing the local elites. The first editions were compiled based on the snowball method, that is, people whom the register authors knew provided names of their acquaintances, who were in turn asked for information about their acquaintances, etc. The name list in the register is repeatedly updated with recourse to the data from applications of candidates in-spe and wide-ranged screening performed by the register committee in clubs, religious organisations and even among neighbours. As one can rocket into the register, one can also plummet out of it by committing a misalliance or a common crime. The committee of *Social Register* scrutinises marriages and divorces in this respect.

The upper class attributes, such as a sense of exclusiveness, the belief in superiority, group solidarity and a sense of distinctive position, are inculcated in long-lasting preparations for the elite roles. The socialisation process involves teaching children to speak a specific language, to exhibit proper manners and to think in right ways. They are also trained in particular forms of conduct, sartorial codes and tastes. These skills and habits are moulded by expensive tutors and in educational travels which pair exploration of foreign customs and cultures with intense study. The daily life of upper-class children is packed with an endless routine of ballet classes, music lessons, tennis and skiing practice and social obligations. The latter involve for example balls, with a debutante ball ushering adolescent girls into the ladies' community and the marriage market.

In the second half of the 19th century, the greatest number of boarding schools were set up in New England (Massachusetts, New Hampshire, Connecticut) with the idea of preventing the offspring of the local elites from mixing with newcomers. Modelled upon English public schools combining educational facilities and dormitories, the system's effectiveness inspires trust proportional to its own conservatism. Students must comply with strict rigours, wear uniforms and ties, play squash and, in some such institutions, address teachers as "masters." *Fortune*'s school ranking has New Hampshire's Saint Grottlesex schools in the top position. One of them, St. Paul's with a campus of 2,000 acres of land and woods, charges $6.8 thousand in annual tuition, has a 1:6.3 teacher-student ratio and runs classrooms of no more than 12 students (Domhoff 1983: 26).

The elitist education system is the most effective way of ensuring the intergenerational continuity of the upper class. As early as at elementary school, closely-knit groups of friends are formed who then go on to study at the same high schools and universities. They spend leisure time together, playing polo, frequenting parties and banquets, and finally choosing spouses. They join student organisations, corporations and fraternities which safeguard them from dwindling into anonymity. To be a Princeton or Harvard student is one thing, and to be a student of the Harvard inhabited by people whose uncles and aunties are also your uncles and aunties is a very different, special thing. The other Harvard is emblematised in the exotic names of fraternities, such as Porcellian, Fly and A.D.; at Yale, their counterparts are Zeta Psi and Delta Kappa Ypsilon.

The Polish Upper Class

There is no upper class in Poland. More than that, even if an upper class comes into being in Poland, it will not be the same as the English upper class. In 1896, Winston Churchill was 2nd lieutenant in the Fourth Queen's Own Hussars stationed near London: "In those days English Society still existed in its old form. It was a brilliant and powerful body," Churchill explains, "with standards of conduct and methods of enforcing them now altogether forgotten. In a very large degree every one knew every one else and who they were. The few hundred great families who had governed England for so many generations and seen her rise to the pinnacle of her glory, were inter-related to an enormous extent by marriage. Everywhere one met friends and kinsfolk. The leading figures in society were in many cases the leading statesmen in Parliament, and also the leading sportsmen on the Turf. Lord Salisbury [the then Prime Minister] was accustomed scrupulously to avoid calling a Cabinet when there was racing in Newmarket [...] In those days the glittering parties at Lansdowne House, Devonshire House or Stafford House comprised all the elements which made a gay and splendid social circle in close relation to the business of Parliament, the hierarchies of Army and Navy, and the policy of the State" (Churchill 2010: 89-90).

While every society has its privileged categories and nurtures its notions of superiority, in democratic systems the "upper classes" is less conspicuous and has less aura of aristocratic grandeur. It is a sheer impossibility to ascertain whether the communist system in Poland would have spawned an upper class of its own had it not collapsed (which it did in 1989). What we do know is that all political crises troubling the communist system from 1956 on robbed the upper governmental echelons of permanence which could potentially have given them legitimacy and social prestige. The party officials with plebeian names were unable to rival, for example, the princely Radziwiłł, and the sparse business people, who counted as the elite of wealth, had hardly any possibilities to parade their affluence and sport it publicly. Consequently, there emerged no privileged social group of incontestable status, strengthened by the in-group bonding, personally acquainted with the ruling elite and influential by itself, additionally basking in historically rooted deference and nostalgic sentiments. The upper class stood no chance of flourishing in the system which was submerged in and promoted mediocrity. The elites of the Polish United Workers' Party (PZPR) resented all things aristocratic and courtly, or even redolent of those.

The most symptomatic and novel aspect of stratification processes after the fall of communism was the rise of the business elite. The specialist journal *Home & Market* publishes estimates of Poland's richest people's wealth. In 2000, the top 500 list was headed by Jan Kulczyk with $1.449 billion, followed by Aleksander Gudzowaty ($1.089 billion), Ryszard Krauze ($675 million) and Zygmunt Solorz ($660 million). With $186 million, Sobiesław Zasada was ranked 13, and Krzysztof Przewrocki from House of Prince (tobacco) owning estimated $171 million ranked 15 (Jasiecki 2001).

With the figures from *Forbes* in mind, let us make two comments. Firstly, the distance between the wealthiest Americans and the wealthiest Poles is striking. Only Kulczyk and Gudzowaty, owning above $1 billion each, would qualify into the top twenty of the American business elite. Admittedly though, falling short of the American achievements in this respect is no reason for shame.

Secondly, Poland has already produced its own financial elite which outdistances the average Pole by millions' worth of wealth. The group consists of big shareholders (such as Kulczyk, Krauze, Zasada or Solorz) and senior managers in the biggest firms and companies. According to the estimates of specialist magazines and business clubs, in 2000 the group oscillated between a few hundred and a few thousand people – about 0.0001% of the total population. The percentage reflects how exclusive this category is even though in terms of income and wealth it still trails far behind its Western counterparts.

In Western democracies, the interests of the upper class are represented by various organisations and in various ways. Empirical studies warn against one-sided demonising of these arrangements. In fact, social classes rarely become a collective actor and certainly do not act as such on daily basis. A vision of the collective rule exercised by the business elite is a fruit of speculative thinking akin to Marxism.

In the United States, the vital interests of the upper class are channelled mainly by the Business Council, a quintessentially elitist association of corporate leaders, heads of research institutes and banking CEOs, whose names are regularly published in *Who is Who in America*. The Business Council members meet the government officials in more or less formal circumstances, receive reports and opinions, and present initiatives and suggestions. The Council convenes in attractive resorts, for example Hot Springs, Virginia, where panel discussions intermingle with sports and social events, creating a productive mix of moods conducive to constructive solutions. Interests can also be served in more institutionalised ways, such as lobbying. In the US Congress, upper-class interests are promoted by the Business Roundtable, an organisation which during the Ford and Carter administrations effectively thwarted consumer protection legislation (Domhoff 1983: 136). The US president uses also consultancy of multiple advisory councils recommending health care, education, economic and social welfare policies.

However, power is most effectively consolidated by governmental appointments. One of the idiosyncrasies of the governing style in Poland is an influx of political officials into private business. Former ministers, statesmen and MPs become corporate chairmen, get selected to supervisory and management boards, acquire substantial shareholdings or set up their own companies. However, there is no reverse migration – from business to government – which distinguishes the Polish experience from that typical of Western countries, where the transfer of business leaders to positions of political power serves as a tried and tested method of the upper class's participation in governance.

In the United States, the senior managerial staff of leading companies forms an integral base of administration and government. In the second half of the 1970s, 28% of CEOs in industrial corporations were members of various advisory bodies of the US government, while the proportion of advisors from small businesses stood at 4%. This reflected an extraordinary eagerness of the big business to engage with the duties of governance (Useem, 1980). The big business had its people accede to the highest positions in the US administration. Harold Brown, the Secretary of the Defence in Carter's cabinet, had been director of a few corporations and president of California Institute of Technology; and Michael Blumenthal, former president of Bendix Corporation, became the Secretary of the Treasury. Commenting on the appointments, journalists pointed out that the government was less tightly associated with the White House than with the Rockefeller Foundation, IBM or Wall Street. The first Secretary of State in the Reagan administration – General Alexander Haig, president of Manhattan Bank, Crown Cork & Seal and Texas Instruments – cut a well-known figure among the Polish TV viewers in the 1980s. Haig's physiognomy left no doubts that America had irrevocably abandoned the kid-glove policy toward the Kremlin, which made him a constant target of propagandist attacks launched by the Polish media. The next Secretary of State, George Schultz, was president of Bechtel

Corporation, one of the world's largest construction companies, and director of Morgan Guaranty Trust. Caspar Weinberger, the Secretary of the Defence, started his career as a lawyer, but in the 1970s was a CEO at Pepsico & Quaker Oats.

In a reformist gesture, the last communist government appointed Mieczysław Wilczek Minister of Industry. Popularly reputed as a very brisk businessman, Wilczek openly admitted to his wealth and kept putting his hard-earned money to productive use, which took some grit in the unpredictable times of waning communism. In post-communist governments, the only popular figure recognisably affiliated with the big business was Ireneusz Sekuła. Sekuła was appointed chairman of the Central Customs Office by Włodzimierz Cimoszewicz, Prime Minister of the coalition government formed by the Democratic Left Alliance and the Polish Peasant Party.

Big owners do not go into politics in Poland. Professional political careers are pursued mostly by the intelligentsia, primarily economists and lawyers (Wasilewski 2000). The government administration does not find the business elite a relevant partner. One reason for this is that the big capitalists are regarded as a yet inadequate economic power; additionally, partnership with them could be rather awkward since no formalised rules are in place for collaboration between government and corporate leaders. Professional lobbying, which offers legal ways of negotiating such issues, is only in a nascent state; and, even more importantly, the junction of business and politics is commonly viewed as a hotbed of corruption. In 2001, the Polish Parliament passed a bill which restrained business involvement of people who perform public functions. The engagement of politicians in economic structures has earned a derogatory name of "political capitalism," accused of corroding governance. The big business financing of politics and the concomitant "loot sharing" practised by political parties have occasioned a surge of charges of public funds appropriation levelled against politicians sitting on supervisory boards of holdings, companies and public health funds.

So, the business elite was practically absent from governmental offices. And as for participation of business people in influential advisory bodies – another very effective and widespread practice of securing the interests of corporate capital in Western countries – that was hardly a sufficient compensation. In the 1990s, a few organisations of shareholders in the biggest companies were founded in Poland. The most influential of them – Business Center Club, Polish Business Round-table (Polska Rada Biznesu) and Polish Confederation of Private Employers (Polska Konfederacja Pracodawców Prywatnych) – are committed to furthering liberal reforms. Actively engaged in promotion and consciousness-raising, they organise seminars to extend contacts and seek to integrate the business milieu by spreading models of life style and conduct. Like in Western countries, representatives of the business world take part in the work of parliamentary commissions, are involved in legal monitoring and submit economic policy projects. They also sit on the Trilateral Commission (Komisja Trójstronna), which was established in 1992 to mediate and conciliate between employers, trade unions and government.

The Polish Business Roundtable follows the model worked out by America's Business Roundtable in having its members associate with policy-makers on private footing in club-like atmosphere regardless of any institutional connections. Founded in 1991-1992, the Polish Business Roundtable and Business Center Club were supposed to provide a site for concocting an upper-class ethos, emulating *esprit de corps* which saturates English and American clubs and integrating the upper class socially. Both charge an initiation fee and, once admitted, the members pay substantial membership fees. The Polish Business Roundtable observes restricted membership rules with eligibility limited to the top executives of large companies with annual proceeds in excess of $10 million and baseline employment above 100.

In Western countries, traditional symbols of the upper class are beginning to take on new forms. Characteristically, the wealthy are starting to embrace liquid forms of ownership, which in practice means that an owner of a huge fortune may dwell in a leased house. The most active and dynamic people, perpetually on the move, live in luxury hotel apartments, hire jewellery and furniture and drive rented cars. In its growing mobility, the upper class resumes the old aristocratic migratory modes which look back to the Middle Ages, when the monarch kept traversing the realm, the capital city was a rather vague notion, and the court settled for a year or two only to hit the road again.

The Ruling Class

In Poland, the idea of founding elite clubs has gained a responsive audience in the up-an-coming big business. Yet the Polish big business falls short of the upper class as it lacks the primary attribute – an intimately-knit informal circle of respectable families and close friends. The genuine upper class presents a maze of posh connections and alliances, boasts a historical lineage and cultivates its heritage. Though important, wealth is inconsequential vis-à-vis social legitimation symbolised by *Social Register* in the USA, the House of Lords in England and a common sentiment for the aristocracy and old families elsewhere. This holds true also for Poland: the already existing fortunes looking to seize ministerial offices in future would still have to strive to gain public recognition.

Society is like a living organism. The organic analogy means that social categories and classes are assigned particular functions instrumental to the survival of the entire social organism. Peasants are supposed to supply food, manual workers produce material goods, the intelligentsia tend to spiritual matters, create symbols and uphold values, the clergy communicate with God, entrepreneurs coordinate, the middle class (if there is any) ensures an equilibrium, and the elites must bear the tasks of governance. The upper class, whose role within this model is hard to pinpoint precisely, is most probably driven by inertia, which does not mean that it serves no purpose altogether. As a component of the social structure, the upper class secures important needs but is not necessarily destined to last for ever.

Let us note that there is no such category in Polish society at present. And as for the future, the upper class cannot be consigned to oblivion, but certainly it has no place in the mainstream of modernisation in market societies. In the 1990s, an international survey called *New Democratic Barometer* sought to establish whether Central-European societies backed the reinstitution of monarchy in their respective states. The findings showed a rather meagre support for the idea. The relatively highest support for it was reported in Romania and Bulgaria, with 18% and 15% of their respective population samples declaring positive opinions about monarchy. In Belarus, which has in fact never even been a sovereign duchy, monarchy was endorsed by 15% of the population, while the project got the least support in Hungary and the Czech Republic, where about 2% of the national samples opted for it. In Poland, the category whishing monarchy to return accounted for 10% of the sample, which placed us at the mid-point of the scale (Rose et al. 1998: 111).

Motivated by my subjective experience of sporadic meetings with the members of Poland's old families, let me share a short reflection on the restoration of the upper classes. The scene is set in an informal meeting, and the *dramatis personae* include interlocutors, the author and X, a female of old Lithuanian pedigree, with a position in Tadeusz Mazowiecki's cabinet, well-known from her TV appearances, at the apex of her popularity. Her well-cared-for face and her slender silhouette a tell-tale sign of body care, when speaking X puts on a blasé face, her eyes lingering on the walls around, never once focusing on the others present or any details. A few people seated round a table are engaged in a laid-back conversation (which the author finds an alleviating circumstance) when X, an offspring of an aristocratic family influentially involved in pre-war politics, starts to expatiate on her daughter's accomplishments in the tones of royalty enlightening the subjects on the crown prince's exploits. At this point, the author will exceptionally use his authorial prerogative of subjectivity to express doubts as to X's adamant confidence that the public hold the old families in admiration and are versed in their kinship affiliations. As the conversation went on, X turned out to believe that, if need be, the aristocracy would be ready to bear the burden of governance and, should that come to pass, the people would roll out the red carpet for them. Not quite sharing X's sentiments, the author wished X had shown more class in reticence and self-control, the sacred standards of the English upper class. The meeting left an ambivalent aftertaste as one was at a loss about what was worse: the hypocrisy of the former regime's dignitaries or the self-righteous smugness of the would-be Lithuanian bulls.

Conclusion: Prospects for the Middle-Class Society in Poland

Whenever a government seeks to rely on a previously observed statistical regularity for control purposes, that regularity will collapse.

Charles Goodhart (economist and statistician)

A dozen years ago, the development of the middle class would daily make headlines of newspapers in Poland. With the middle class becoming a highly charged political issue, the government would be called to account on policies for its progress. As for grassroots initiatives, the renewal of the middle class was promoted by a citizen group associated with the now non-existent weekly *Cash*. The group's spontaneous activity reached its apogee in 1995 with the foundation of the Polish Middle Class Registration Committee (Komisja Rejestracyjna Polska Klasa Średnia), which issued membership certificates to candidates who met the following criteria: had at least secondary education, owned a car and earned at least PLN 1,500 monthly (a relatively small sum at the time). The enthusiastic activists magically believed that creation of social structures was a viable project and saw it as a crucial development in progress. Although the novice enthusiasm has waned and other problems are talk of the day now, the middle class is not doomed to sink into obscurity of archival scrolls. In May 2001, the election banners of the Freedom Union (Unia Wolności) read "A strong middle class means strong Poland." That veritably pioneering ferment brought "the middle class" to the centre of the political stage, symbolically at least, and kindled hopes for the middle class to evolve into the most important constituency, like in the USA or England.

The propagandist context has been as important to the formation of the middle class as its objective efforts. Let me remind that throughout this book the phenomena related to the development of this category in Poland have usually been explained in terms of objective rules. The middle-class society has served as a point of reference which helps define the distance between Poland and the developed market systems. Making such a comparison, we might have used also such concepts as "information," "consumer," "post-industrial," "equal opportunity," or "risk society" proposed and popularised by Galbraith (1967), McClelland

(1967), Bela (1976), Beck (1992) and other researchers. I opted for the "middle class" because it combines a few important dimensions.

Recapitulating, we could say that over the dozen years since the onset of the systemic transformation, the distance between Poland and developed Western countries has shrunk slightly. The most important factor was a steady increase in consumption and real incomes. Poland's urban population could choose from attractive consumer goods, ranging from a hamburger at McDonald's to the latest makes of Ford or BMW. Even the lower classes are the beneficiaries of political changes. Supermarkets offer merchandise which can impart a sense of comfort even to the poorest. It is 2002 and an entire epoch has passed since Poland saw the end of the planned economy. And to think that after the marital law was proclaimed by the communist government in December 1981 the only commodity in abundance in shops was vinegar!

The growth in affluence was concurrent with changes in the stratification system. In the 1990s, the executives and the non-technical intelligentsia climbed to the top, recording an unprecedented upward mobility. Like in middle-class societies, a gap started to open between the relatively best paid managers and experts, on the one hand, and lower-ranked white collars on the other, with workers slipping down to the bottom regions of the social hierarchy.

In the 1990s, the university degree started to exert a greater impact on access to socio-economic positions. For employers, education became an indicator of employees' competence, responsibility and self-discipline. The role of executive positions grew, and incomes of private business people systematically declined. Consequently, if educational capital and managerial roles became essentially important, the small ownership was losing its impact. This is a symptomatic trend, as similar tendencies have been observed in the developed market systems over recent decades.

The middle-class society is made up of individuals who uphold a shared set of values and attitudes. In Western countries, many constitutive traits of "the spirit of capitalism" – such as profit-orientation, dedication to work and daily austerity – have been toppled by a desire for a life of luxury. Nevertheless, the core attributes of liberalism, tolerance and self-reliance have not been dented and stand tall as pillars of democracy and market relations. In Poland, the decade of the 1990s saw a series of alterations in value systems which were inauspicious for the development of the middle class. Firstly, the acceptance for the state interventionist policies increased discernibly. Secondly, people continued to declare low tolerance for homosexual relationships, marital infidelity and premarital sex. Perhaps even more distressing for the development of the middle class in Poland is the reluctance to pursue self-reliant life careers common even among the intelligentsia and owners, regarded as the founding fathers of the nascent middle class.

These insights suggest that capitalism is being built in Poland against the prevalent social moods. Many changes come across as coercion, which was not exactly envisaged in 1989, when the market rules and relationships were launched. The sense of coercion starts with such basic things as company dress-codes and luggage regulations for business trips. The code at Ernst & Young, for example, allows a light make-up for women, with a recommendation to subtly accentuate the eyes so important in contact with customers, but bans low necklines, sweeping and transparent fabrics and polka-dot patterns. The male Ernst & Young staff are advised not to wear striped and check suits and short socks. International real estate consultants Healey & Baker forbid men to wear jumpers, text T-shirts and jeans. Thankfully, employees are not made to wear Chinese-style navy-blue overalls, but they are instructed how to dress and have the imperative of attractive uniformity made clear to them.

Middle-class societies evolved based on roles which enforced self-reliance, status-seeking, and readiness to fight for a better position. In Western Europe, these drives clashed with the feudal habits and had to push their way through more hurdles than in the USA. In Poland, they fare even worse. For one thing, Poland has never known an ideology akin to the American Dream, which instils faith in equal opportunity and unlimited possibilities lying open to the talented and the resourceful. More poignantly, it has not sunk in yet that such attitudes are a matter of necessity rather than of choice because capitalism deals out success (or failure) irrespective of individual preferences.

Success orientations will not thrive in Poland unless society grants them a moral sanction by censuring inertia and denying respect to those who fail to face up to challenges. The "Polish Dream," like the American one, must give a cautionary thrust to self-discipline. This, however, does not seem to be happening naturally. One reason for it is that this dream has a moralising and spurious ring to it even for rational people. This different approach is illustrated in surveys which included several countries representing various economies and political systems: while in England, the Netherlands and the USA the respondents indicated hard work and personal abilities as the most important factors in wealth, an average Pole ascribed wealth to dishonesty, unfair fate and the unjust social system (Alwin et al. 1993).

Middle-class Americans are habituated into an orderly career pattern, in which a degree from a good university is to be followed by a good job. People with an upgrading urge, compulsively putting their success on display, are valued and promoted. The middle-class society counts on investors and, primarily, on young managers and professionals who can afford a house and a summer house, own two cars, sport a yacht and regularly revamp their apartments in order to keep up with their neighbours, if not to outclass them. The exact data for Poland are not available, but the signs of neighbours' success are far more likely to be looked at with a jaundiced eye in these parts.

Poles are extensively tested for their capacity to deal with insurance, the stock market, the mortgage and other ownership forms. We might resent that, but we have no other choice. Those who wish a comfortable flat, a good car and exotic holidays must be more appreciative of individual achievement than ever before. The middle-class society is, in all probability, the most arduous path of development, but for those who want to develop, it may indeed be the only path to follow.

Bibliography

Adamski W., K. Jasiewicz, A. Rychard (eds.), 1986, *Polacy '84. Dynamika konfliktu i konsensusu. Raport z badania*, Uniwersytet Warszawski, Warszawa.

Alger H. Jr., 1962, *Ragged Dick and Mark the Match Boy*, New York.

Alwin D. et al., 1993, "Comparative Referential Structures, System Legitimacy, and Justice Sentiments," in: Kluegel J. R., Mason D. S. i Wegener B. (eds.), *Social Justice and Political Change: Public Opinion in Capitalist and Post-Communist States*, [np], pp. 109–130.

Amory C., 1960, *Who Killed Society?*, Harper & Rows Publ., New York.

Anderson P., 1992, *English Questions*, Verso, London.

Aron, Raymond, 2011 (1957), *The Opium of the Intellectuals*, Transaction Publishers, New Brunswick.

Baltzell D. E., 1958, *Philadelphia Gentlemen. The Making of a National Upper Class*, The Free Press, Glencoe.

Baltzell D. E., 1991, *The Protestant Establishment Revisited*, Transaction Publ., New Brunswick.

Beck U., 1992, *Risk Society: Towards a New Modernity*, Sage, London.

Bell D., 1976, *The Cultural Contradictions of Capitalism*, Heinneman, London.

Bellah R. N. et al., 1986, *Habits of the Heart: Individualism and Commitment in American Life*, Harper and Rows Publ., New York.

Benda J., 1927, *Le trahison des clercs*, Paris.

Berle A., C.G. Means, *The Modern Corporation and Private Property*, Harcourt Brace & World, New York.

Blau P., O.D. Duncan, 1967, *The American Occupational Structure*, Academic Press, New York.

Boorstin D. J., 1995, *Amerykanie. Fenomen demokracji* [The Americans: The Democratic Experience], Bellona, Warszawa.

Borucki A., 1994, "Inteligencja polska przed transformacją systemu," *Kultura i Społeczeństwo* 1.

Borucki A., 1994, *Polska inteligencja współczesna*, Wydawnictwo IFiS PAN, Warszawa.

Bourdieu P., 1985, *Distinction: A Social Critique of the Judgment of Taste*, Routledge, London.

Brzozowski S., 1910, *Legenda Młodej Polski*, Lwów.

Carr-Saunders A. M., P.A. Wilson, 1933, *Professions*, Clarendon Press, Oxford.

Cash, 1995a, "Rejestracja Stowarzyszenia Polska Klasa Średnia," *Cash* 50, p. 13.

Cash, 1995b, "Program Stowarzyszenia Polska Klasa Średnia," *Cash* 51–52, p. 22.

CBOS, 1998, *Opinie Polaków o własnej pracy*, Biuletyn, Centrum Badania Opinii Społecznej, Warszawa.

CBOS, 2001, *Rozumienie, akceptacja społeczna i ocena funkcjonowania polskiej demokracji*, Komunikat z badań, August, Warszawa.

Chałasiński J., 1948, *Społeczna genealogia inteligencji polskiej*, PWN, Warszawa.

Chinoy E., 1995, *Automobile Workers and the American Dream*, Doubleday.

Churchill, Winston, *My Early Life: 1874-1904*. Simon and Shuster, 2010.

Cichomski B., P. Morawski, 1995, *Polski Generalny Sondaż Społeczny. Skumulowany komputerowy zbiór danych*, Instytut Studiów Społecznych, Uniwersytet Warszawski, Warszawa.

Cohen J., P. Cohen, 1983, *Applied Multiple Regression/Correlation Analysis in Behavioral Sciences*, Lawrence Erlbaum, Hillsdale, New Jersey.

Czarnowski P., 1997, "Dzisiaj i za kilka lat," in: *Gazeta Wyborcza*: „Public Relations" Supplement, 4–5 April.

Dahrendorf R., 1959, *Class and Class Conflict in Industrial Society*, Stanford University Press, Stanford.

Dahrendorf R., 1993, *Nowoczesny konflikt społeczny* [The Modern Social Conflict], Czytelnik, Warszawa.

Daszyński I., 1957, *Pamiętniki*, Vol. 1, Książka i Wiedza, Warszawa.

Davis J. A., 1982, "Achievement variables and class cultures: family, schooling and forty-nine dependent variables in the cumulative GSS," *American Sociological Review* 47, pp. 569–659.

Derber C., 1996, *The Wilding of America*, St. Martin's Press, New York.

Domański H., 1986, "Dobór i struktura próby," in: W. Adamski, K. Jasiewicz, A. Rychard (eds.), *Polacy '84. Dynamika konfliktu i konsensusu. Raport z badania*, Uniwersytet Warszawski, Warszawa.

Domański H., 1994, *Społeczeństwa klasy średniej*, Wydawnictwo IFiS PAN, Warszawa.

Domański H., 1996, *Na progu konwergencji. Stratyfikacja społeczna w krajach Europy Środkowo-Wschodniej*, Wydawnictwo IFiS PAN, Warszawa.

Domański H., 1997, "Mobilność i hierarchie stratyfikacyjne," in: H. Domański, A. Rychard (eds.), *Elementy nowego ładu*, Wydawnictwo IFiS PAN, Warszawa.

Domański H., 1999, *Prestiż*, Monografie Fundacji na Rzecz Nauki Polskiej, Seria Humanistyczna, Funna, Wrocław.

Domański H., 2000a, *Hierarchie i bariery społeczne w latach 90-tych*, Instytut Spraw Publicznych, Warszawa.

Domański H., 2000b, "Zamiast zakończenia," in: H. Domański, A. Ostrowska, A. Rychard (eds.), *Jak żyją Polacy?*, Wydawnictwo IFiS PAN, Warszawa.

Domański H., A. Dukaczewska, 1997, "Samodzielność i chęć polegania na sobie," in: H. Domański, A. Rychard (eds.), *Elementy nowego ładu*, Wydawnictwo IFiS PAN, Warszawa.

Domhoff G. W., 1967, *Who Rules America?*, Englewood Cliffs, N. J.: Prentice Hall.

Domhoff G. W., 1974, *The Bohemian Grove and Other Retreats*, Harper & Rows Publ., New York.

Domhoff G. W., 1983, *Who Rules America Now?*, Simon & Schuster, New York.

Donohue W. A., 1990, *The New Freedom: American Individualism and Collectivism in the Social Lives of Americans*, Transaction Publishers, Brunswick and London.

Dore R., 1992, "Sovereign individuals," in: J. A. Hall J. A., C. Jarvie (eds.), *Transition to Modernity: Essays on Power, Wealth and Belief*, Cambridge University Press, Cambridge, pp. 167–184.

Dunleavy P., C.T. Husbands, 1985, *British Democracy at the Crossroads: Voting and Party Competition in the 1980s*, Allen and Unwin, London.

Dye T. R., 1978, "Oligarchic Tendencies in National Policy-Making: the Role of the Private Policy-Planning Organisations," *Journal of Politics* 40, pp. 309–331.

Dye T. R., 1995, *Who's Running America?: The Clinton Years*, 6th ed., Englewood Cliffs, N. J.: Prentice-Hall.

Ehrenreich B., 1992, *Fear of Falling: The Inner Life of the Middle Class*, Harper Perennial, New York.

Erikson R., J. H. Goldthorpe, 1992, *The Constant Flux: A Study of Class Mobility in Industrial Societies*, Clarendon Press, Oxford.

Etzioni A., 1994, *The Spirit of Community: The Reinvention of American Society*, Crown, New York.

Fee J. et al., 1981, *Young Catholics: A Report to the Knights of Columbus*, Sadlier, Los Angeles.

Galbraith K., 1967, *The New Industrial State*, Hamish Hamilton, London.

Gans H. J., 1988, *Middle American Individualism: The Future of Liberal Democracy*, The Free Press, New York.

Gardawski J., 2001, *Powracająca klasa*, Wydawnictwo IFiS PAN, Warszawa.

Gestern A., 2000, "Droga do kariery nad Wisłą," *Rzeczpospolita*, 13 December, 290 (5760). "Moja Kariera" Supplement: 6.

Giza-Poleszczuk A., M. Marody, A. Rychard, 2000, *Strategie i system*, Wydawnictwo IFiS PAN, Warszawa.

Goban-Klas T., 1997, *Public Relations*, Business Press, Warszawa.

Goldthorpe J. H. et al., 1969, *The Affluent Worker*, Cambridge University Press, Cambridge.

Goldthorpe J. H., G. Marshall, 1992, "The Promising Future of Class Analysis: A Response to Recent Critiques," *Sociology* 26, pp. 381–400.

Gombrowicz, W., 2012, *Diary*, trans. Lillian Vallee, Yale University Press.

Gouldner A., 1979, *The Future of Intellectuals and the Rise of the New Class*, Seabury, New York.

Guttsman W. L., 1969, *The English Ruling Class*, Weidenfeld and Nicholson, London.

Hacker A., 1998, *Money: Who Has How Much and Why*, Simon & Schuster, New York.

Hampden-Turner Ch., A. Trompenaars, *Siedem kultur kapitalizmu* [The Seven Cultures of Capitalism], Dom Wydawniczy ABC, Warszawa.

Harrington M., 1983, *The Politics at God's Funeral: The Spiritual Crisis of Western Civilisation*, Holt, Rinehart and Winston, New York.

Hickox M., 1995, "The English middle-class debate," *British Journal of Sociology* 46, pp. 311–323.

Hollingshead A., F. Redlich, 1958, *Social Class and Mental Illness: A Community Study*, John Wiley & Sons, New York.

Horney K., 1998, *Neurotyczna osobowość naszych czasów* [The Neurotic Personality of Our Time], Wydawnictwo Rebis, Poznań.

Hyman H., 1954, "The Value Systems of Different Classes," in: R. Bendix, S. M. Lipset (eds.), *Class, Status and Power: Social Stratification in Comparative Perspective*, Free Press, Glencoe, Ill.

Inglehart R., 1997, *Modernisation and Postmodernisation: Cultural, Economic and Political Change in 43 Societies*, Princeton University Press, Princeton.

Inglehart R., M. Basanez, A. Moreno, 1998, *Human Values and Beliefs: A Cross-Cultural Sourcebook*, University of Chicago Press, Ann Arbor 1998.

Jasiecki K., 2001, *Elita prywatnego biznesu, Formowanie się nowych aktorów transformacji w Polsce*, Wydawnictwo IFiS PAN, Warszawa.

Jaźwińska E., 1999, "Przedsiębiorcy na tle innych grup społeczno-zawodowych w Polsce," in: *Przedsiębiorcy jako grupa społeczna*, Warszawa, pp. 9–28.

Jedlicki J., 2000, "Historia inteligencji polskiej w kontekście europejskim," *Kultura i Społeczeństwo* 2, pp. 141–162.

Jefferson T., 1943, *The Complete Jefferson*, S. K. Padover (ed.), New York 1943.

Keat R., 1991, "Introduction," in: R. Keat, N. Abercrombie (eds.), *Enterprise Culture*, Routledge, London, pp. 1–11.

Kerbo H. R., 1996, *Social Stratification and Inequality*, The McGraw-Hill, New York.

Kocka J., 1997, *O społecznej historii Niemiec*, Wydawnictwo Poznańskie, Poznań.

Kohn M., C. Schooler, 1986, *Struktura społeczna a osobowość*, PWN, Warszawa.

Kurczewski J., 1998, "Rozważania nad strukturą społecznych emancypacji," *Studia Socjologiczne* 2, pp. 69–88.

Lamont M., 1992, *Money, Morals & Manners. The Culture of the French and the American Upper-Middle Class*, The University of Chicago Press, Chicago and London.

Lane R. E., 2000, *The Loss of Happiness in Market Democracies*, Yale University Press, London.

Lasch Ch., 1982, *The Culture of Narcissism: American Life in an Age of Diminishing Expectations*, Norton, New York.

Lash S., J. Urry, 1987, *The End of Organized Capitalism*, Polity, Cambridge.

Laswell H. D., 1952, *The Comparative Studies of Elites: An Introduction and Bibliography*, Stanford University Press, Stanford.

Lerner M., 1961, *America as a Civilisation*, Simon & Schuster, New York.

Lipset S. M., 1961, *Political Man: The Social Bases of Politics*, Baltimore, MD: Johns Hopkins University, 1961.

Lockwood D., 1958, *The Blackcoated Worker: A Study in Class Consciousness*, Unwin, London.

Lodge, David., 1986, *Out of the Shelter*, Penguin Books, London.

Lynd R., H. Lynd, 1929, *Middletown*, Harcourt Brace Jovanowich, New York.

Lynn K. S., 1955, *The Dream of Success: A Study of the Modern American Imagination*, Boston.

Marcinkowski A., 1996, "Drobni przedsiębiorcy i horyzonty kultury organizacyjnej," in: A. Marcinkowski (ed.), *Kapitalizm po polsku. Przedsiębiorca, organizacja, kultura*, Kraków.

Marshall G., 1982, *In Search of the Spirit of Capitalism: An Essay on Max Weber's Protestant Ethic Thesis*, Hutchinson, London.

Marshall G., 1997, *Repositioning Class: Social Inequality in Industrial Societies*, London.

Marshall G. et al., 1988, *Social Class in Modern Britain*, Unwin Hyman, Ltd., London.

Martin B., 1995, "Symbols, Codes and Cultures," in: P. Joyce (ed.), *Class*, Oxford University Press, Oxford.

McClelland D. C., 1961, *The Achievement Society*, Free Press, New York.

McLeod J., 1987, *Ain't No Makin' It: Leveled Aspirations in a Low-Income Neighbourhood*, Westview Press, Boulder, Colo.

Mead M., 1942, *And Keep Your Powder Dry: An Anthropologist Look at America*, Morrow & Co., New York.

Mills C. W., 1951, *White Collar: The American Middle Classes*, Oxford University Press.

Mintz B., 1975, "The President's Cabinet, 1897–1972: A Contribution to the Power Structure Debate," *Insurgent Sociologist* 5, pp. 131–148.

Mizerski S., 1996, "Dwunasty kilometr," *Polityka* 16, pp. 92–95.

Mokrzycki E., 2001, *Bilans niesentymentalny*, Wydawnictwo IFiS PAN, Warszawa.

Morikawa H., 1992, *Zaibatsu: The Rise and Fall of Family Enterprise Groups in Japan*, Tokyo University Press, Tokyo.

Mosier R. D., 1947, *Making the American Mind*, New York 1947.

Newby H., 1977, *The Deferential Worker*, Penguin, Harmondsworth.

Nowakowska M., 1977, *Postawy społeczne wobec problemu kształcenia*, Ossolineum, Wrocław.

Offe K., 1985, *Disorganized Capitalism: Contemporary Transformations of Work and Politics*, The MIT Press, Cambridge, Massachussets.

Offe K., 1961, *Varieties of Transition: The East European and East German Experience*, Polity Press, Oxford.

Orwell G., 1961, *Collected Essays*, Secker & Warburg, London.

Ostrowska A., 1997, *Styl życia a zdrowie*, Wydawnictwo IFiS PAN, Warszawa.

Packard V., 1962, *The Status Seekers*, [np] Pelican Books, 1962.

Pakulski J., M. Waters, 1996, *The Death of Class*, Sage, London.

Parkin F., 1979, *Marxism and Class Theory: A Bourgeois Critique*, Tavistock, London.

Pipes R., 1990, *Rosja carów* [Russia under the Old Regime], Krąg, Warszawa.

Quirk W. J., R.R. Bridwell, 1992, *Abandoned: The Betrayal of the American Middle Class Since World War II*, Madison Books, Lanham.

Reykowski J., 1992, "Kolektywizm i indywidualizm jako kategorie opisu zmian społecznych i mentalności," *Przegląd Psychologiczny* 2, pp. 147–171.

Riesman D., 1971, *Samotny tłum* [The Lonely Crowd], PWN, Warszawa.

Roemer J., 1982, *A General Theory of Exploitation and Class*, Harvard University Press, Cambridge.

Rose R., Mishler, Ch. Haerpfer, 1998, *Democracy and Its Alternatives: Understanding Post-Communist Societies*, Polity Press, Oxford.

Rotter J. B., 1966, "Generalized Expectancies for Internal Versus External Control of Reinforcement," *Psychological Monographs: General & Applied* 80(1), pp. 1-28.

Rubin L., 1992, *World of Pain: Life in the Working Class Family*, Basic Books, New York.

Rubinstein W. D., 1993, *Capitalism, Culture, and Decline in Britain 1750–1990*, Routledge, London.

"Płace w Polsce '2000," 2001, *Rzeczpospolita*, „Moja Kariera" Supplement, 3 January, no. 2 (575): D-D4.

Sachs G., 1993, *Poland's Jump to the Market*, Unwin Hyman, London.

Saunders R., 1990, *A Nation of Home Owners*, Unwin Hyman, London.

Sawiński Z., H. Domański, 1995, "Polska Socjologiczna Klasyfikacja Zawodów: PSKZ – 1995. Propozycja badawcza," *Ask* 2, pp. 77–94.

Sawiński Z., M. Stasińska, 1986, *Przemiany w oddziaływaniu czynników pochodzenia na dwóch progach selekcji międzyszkolnej*, Zeszyt 42 Zespołu Badań Socjologicznych nad Problemami Oświaty, Instytut Socjologii Uniwersytetu Warszawskiego, Warszawa.

Schmoller G., 1897, *Was verstehen wir unter dem Mittelstand?*, Vandenhoeck und Ruprecht, Gottingen.

Schumpeter J. A., 1995 [1943], *Kapitalizm, socjalizm, demokracja* [Capitalism, Socialism and Democracy], PWN, Warszawa.

Scott J. P., 1993, *Who Rules in Britain?* Polity Press, Cambridge.

Scott J. P., 1997, *Corporate Business and Capitalist Classes*, Oxford University Press, Oxford.

Seeley J. R., R. A. Sim, E. W. Loosley, 1956, *Crestwood Heights: A Study of the Culture of Suburban Life*, Basic Books, New York.

Sennett R., 1998, *The Corrosion of Character: The Personal Consequences of Work in the New Capitalism*, W.W. Norton & Company, New York.

Sewell W. H., A. O. Haller, G. W. Ohlendorf, 1970, "The Educational and Early Occupational Stats Attainment Process: Replication and Revisions," *American Sociological Review* 35, pp. 1014–1027.

Sewell W. H., A. O. Haller, A. Portes, 1969, "The Educational and Early Occupational Attainment Process," *American Sociological Review* 34 (1969), pp. 851–861.

Sewell W. H., R. M. Hauser, 1975, *Education, Occupation and Earnings: Achievement in the Early Career*, Academic Press, New York.

Sewell W. H., R. M. Hauser, W. Wolf, 1979, *Sex, Schooling, and Occupational Status*, University of Wisconsin-Madison (mimeo).

Shavit Y., H.-P. Blossfeld (eds.), 1993, *Persistent Inequality: Changing Educational Attainment in Thirteen Countries*, Westview Press, Boulder.

Shaw G. B., 1884, *Second Fabian Tract*, London.

Skidelsky A., 1999, *Świat po komunizmie* [The World after Communism], Znak, Warszawa.

Słomczyński K. (ed.), 2000, *Social Patterns of Being Political. The Initial Phase of the Post-Communist Transition in Poland*, Wydawnictwo IFiS PAN, Warszawa.

Słomczyński K. M. et al., 1996, *Struktura społeczna a osobowość*, Wydawnictwo IFiS PAN, Warszawa.

Sorokin P., 1959 [1927], *Social and Cultural Mobility*, The Free Press, New York.

Stark D., 1992, "The Great Transformation? Social Change in Eastern Europe," *Contemporary Sociology* 21.

Suchar M., 2000, "Menedżerowie przyszłości," *Rzeczpospolita* 27 December, no. 300: p. F2.

Sztompka P., 2000, "The ambivalence of social change. Triumph or trauma?" *Polish Sociological Review* (131) no. 3, pp. 275–290.

Thatcher M., 1993, *The Downing Street Years*, Harper Collins Publishers, London.

Titkow A., 1997, "Poczucie kontroli nad zdarzeniami w latach 1984–1995," in: H. Domański, A. Rychard (eds.), *Elementy nowego ładu*, Wydawnictwo IFiS PAN, Warszawa.

Tocqueville A. de, 1954, *Democracy in America*, Vintage, New York.

Treiman D. J., 1977, *Occupational Prestige in Comparative Perspective*, Academic Press, New York.

Trollope A., 1978 [1883], *An Autobiography*, ed. B.A. Booth, University of California Press, Berkeley, Los Angeles, London.

Useem M., 1980, "Which business leaders help govern?" in: W. Domhoff (ed.), *Power Structure Research*, Sage Publications, Beverly Hills, pp. 199–225.

Vanneman R., L. W. Cannon, 1987, *The American Perception of Class*, Temple University Press, Philadelphia.

Warner W. L. et al., 1949, *Democracy in Jonesville*, Harper & Brothers, New York.

Warner W. L., P. S. Lunt, 1941, *The Social Life of a Modern Community*, Yankee City Series, Vol. 1, Yale University Press, New Haven.

Warner W. L., M. Meeker, K. Eells, 1949, *Social Class in America*, Chicago.

Warner W. L., J. Abegglen, 1955, *Big Business Leaders in America*, Harper, New York.

Wasilewski J., 2000, "Polish post-transitional elite," in: J. Frentzel-Zagórska, J. Wasilewski (eds.), *The Second Generation of Democratic Elites in Central and Eastern Europe*, Institute of Political Studies, Warszawa, pp. 197–216.

Weber M., 1994 [1905], *Etyka protestancka a duch kapitalizmu* [The Protestant Ethic and the Spirit of Capitalism], trans., Test, Lublin.

Wenzel M., K. Zagórski, 2001, *Postawy wobec wolnego rynku i demokracji w Polsce i Niemczech*, Komunikat z badań, CBOS, Warszawa.

Wesołowski W., 1995, "Procesy klasotwórcze w teoretycznej perspektywie," in: A. Sułek, J. Styk (eds.), *Ludzie i instytucje. Stawanie się ładu społecznego*, Wydawnictwo Uniwersytetu Marii Curie-Skłodowskiej, Lublin.

Wraxall, 1800, *Memoirs of the courts of Berlin, Dresden, Warsaw and Vienna, in the years 1777, 1778, and 1779*. Vol.2. (2nd edition), London.

Wright E. O., 1996, "The continuing relevance of class analysis – Comments," *Theory and Society* 25, pp. 693–716.

Wuthnow R., 1996, *Poor Richard's Principle: Recovering the American Dream through Moral Dimension of Work, Business and Money*, Princeton University Press, Princeton.

Young M., P. Willmott, 1957, *Family and Kinship in East London*, Routledge & Kegan Paul, London.

Ziółkowski M., 2000, *Przemiany wartości i interesów społeczeństwa polskiego*, Wydawnictwo Fundacji Humaniora, Poznań.

Zipp J. F., 1992, "Social class and liberalism," *Sociological Forum* 1, pp. 301–329.

Index of Names

Studies in Social Sciences, Philosophy and History of Ideas

Edited by Andrzej Rychard

www.peterlang.com